The Blessed
of
the Holy Pr
Muḥammad[sa]
and the Caricatures

Friday Sermons Delivered
by Ḥaḍrat Mirzā Masroor
Aḥmad, Khalīfatul Masīḥ V[aba],
Imam Jamā'at-e-Aḥmadiyya

(Friday Sermons Delivered by Ḥaḍrat Mirzā Masroor Aḥmad, Khalīfatul Masīḥ V[aba], Imam Jamā'at-e-Aḥmadiyya)

Translated into English by: Shermeen Butt

Checked and Revised by: Dr. Karimullah Zirvi and
Munir-ud-Din Shams

First Published in UK in 2006

Published by:

Islam International Publications Ltd.
"Islamabad"
Sheephatch Lane
Tilford, Surrey GU10 2AQ, UK

Composed by: Dr. Karimullah Zirvi

Printed in the UK at: CPI Bath

Raqeem Press
Tilford, Surrey

ISBN: 1 85372 913 2

TABLE OF CONTENTS

TRANSLITERATION ix

GLOSSARY xiii

FOREWORD xxi

1. Friday Sermon delivered on 10th February, 2006 1

Reaction of the Muslim world to the publication of the most obnoxious caricatures in Denmark and other Western countries 4

Comments made by certain fair-minded observers 6

Improper reaction by certain Muslim leaders provides an opportunity for the opponents to defame Islam 8

The way an Aḥmadī should react 10

The Promised Messiah[as] came to defend Islam and the Holy Prophet[sa] against conspiracies 11

Enlighten the excellences of the Holy Prophet's[sa] personality and character to the world 14

The immediate response of the Ahmadiyya Muslim Community at the publication of the caricatures 18

Aḥmadī youth should enter the field of Journalism 20

Flag burning or demolition will not establish the honour of the Holy Prophet[sa] 22

Turn your anguish into prayers and invoke blessings upon the Holy Prophet[sa], in abundance 23

2. Friday Sermon delivered on 17th February, 2006 29

Injuring the sentiments of others is neither democracy, nor freedom of conscience 32

Persistent activities intended to blaspheme the Holy Prophet[sa] will incite the Wrath of God Almighty 33

How Aḥmadīs should react under such circumstances 33

The followers of the Promised Messiah[as] will establish the glory of Islam and the sanctity of the Holy Prophet[sa] 34

True meanings of the word *"Nuzūl-e-Masīḥ"*, some of the achievements of the Promised

Messiah[as], and arguments in support of his truth 35

Meaning of the term, "Masīḥ-e-Mau'ūd[as] (the Promised Messiah) will distribute treasures" 38

Explanation of the terms, "Breaking of the Cross" and "Killing of the Swine" 40

The Promised Messiah's advent had to be from *Ummat-e-Muslimah* 43

Masīḥ and Mahdi are two names of the same person; abolition of religious wars by Masīḥ-e-Mau'ūd[as] 45

The sworn testimony of the Promised Messiah[as] that he has been appointed by God Almighty 48

Heavenly signs in support of the Promised Messiah[as] 50

Allah, the Almighty has promised to establish love of the Promised Messiah[as] in the hearts of the people and make his sect dominant over all other sects 54

3. Friday Sermon delivered on 24th February, 2006 61

Double-standards of the Western countries and

newspapers 65

The extremely pitiful plight of Muslims 66

The real cause of Muslim's fragmentation and weakness is their disobedience of the Holy Prophet[sa] and refusal to accept the Promised Messiah 68

The real way of supplicating and receiving blessings 69

Triumph shall come only through prayers 82

The only way to restore the lost glory of Islam is to make an effort, after entering the fold of the community of the Promised Messiah[as] 84

4. Friday Sermon delivered on 3rd March, 2006 91

Publication of the false and baseless news in the newspaper, the *'Jang'* (London), is a provocative and mischievous act 94

I say to the fabricator of this false news, "It is entirely a big lie, and I invoke the curse of Allah on liars by saying: *la'natullāhi 'alal kādhibīn.*" 99

Jamā'at Aḥmadiyya's efforts and reaction to the mischief of caricatures 100

Promised Messiah's[as] love of the Holy Prophet[sa] 102

Muslim Governments should not succumb to the cunning plans of the selfish mullāhs and other elements 104

The gist of the teachings of the Promised Messiah[as] 105

The grand status of the Holy Prophet[sa] in the sight of the Promised Messiah[as] 111

The reality of the issue of Jihad with the sword 114

There will be a full inquiry of the false news and the disguesting conspiracy so that the real aims could be elicited 117

5. Friday Sermon delivered on 10th March, 2006 123

Anti-Islamic activities of certain Muslim groups help non-Muslims in their attacks against Islam 125

Beautiful teachings of Islam with regard to good treatment of non-Muslims 126

Exemplary good behaviour of the Holy Prophet[sa] compared to the excesses and tyranny of the infidels of Mecca and the enemies of Islam 126

Islam did not spread through the force of the

sword. Rather, it spread through good moral behaviour, and the Islamic teachings of freedom of conscience and creed 130

Practical examples of the conduct of the Holy Prophet[sa] with regard to establishment of human values and religious tolerance 140

TRANSLITERATION

In transliterating Arabic words we have followed the following system adopted by the Royal Asiatic Society.

ا at the beginning of a word, pronounced as *a*, *i*, *u*

preceded by a very slight aspiration, like *h* in the English word 'honour'.

ث *th*, pronounced like th in the English word 'thing'.

ح *ḥ*, a guttural aspirate, stronger than h.

خ *kh*, pronounced like the Scotch *ch* in 'loch'.

ذ *dh*, pronounced like the English *th* in 'that'.

ص *ṣ*, strongly articulated s.

ض *ḍ*, similar to the English th in 'this'.

ط *ṭ*, strongly articulated palatal t.

ظ *ẓ*, strongly articulated z.

ع ', a strong guttural, the pronunciation of which must be learnt by the ear.

غ *gh*, a sound approached very nearly in the *r 'grasseye'* in French, and in the German *r*. It requires the muscles of the throat to be in the gargling position whilst pronouncing it.

ق q, a deep guttural k sound.

ء ’, a sort of catch in the voice.

Short vowels are represented by *a* for ـَـ (like *u* in 'bud'); *i* for ـِـ (like *i* in 'bid'); u for ـُـ (like *oo* in 'wood'); the long vowels by *ā* for ـَا or آ (like *a* in 'father'); ī for ـِى or ـٖـ (like *ee* in 'deep'); *ai* for ـَى (like *i* in 'site'); *ū* for ـُو (like *oo* in 'root'); *au* for ـَو (resembling *ou* in 'sound').

Please note that in transliterated words the letter 'e' is to be pronounced as in prey which rhymes with 'day'; however the pronunciation is flat without the element of English diphthong. If in Urdu and Persian word 'e' is lengthened a bit more it is transliterated as 'ei' to be pronounced as 'ei' in 'feign' without the element of diphthong thus 'کے' is transliterated as 'Kei'. For the nasal sound of 'n' we have used the symbol 'ñ'. Thus Urdu word 'میں' would be transliterated as 'meiñ'.

The consonants not included in the above list have the same phonetic value as in the principal languages of Europe.

We have not transliterated Arabic, Persian or Urdu words which have become part of English language, e.g., Islam, Imam, Mahdi, Qur’an, Hijra, Ramadan, Hadith, Zakat,

Sharia, ulema, umma, sunna, kafir, pukka etc.

For quotes straight commas (straight quotes) are used to differentiate them from the curved commas used in the system of transliteration, ‘ for ع, and ’ for ء. Commas as punctuation marks are used according to the normal usage.

The name of Muḥammad[sa], the Holy Prophet of Islam, has been followed by the symbol [sa], which is an abbreviation for the salutation *Ṣallallāhu ‘Alaihi Wasallam* (may peace and blessings of Allah be upon him). The names of other Prophets and Messengers are followed by the symbol [as], an abbreviation for *‘Alaihissalām* (on whom be peace). The actual salutations have not generally been set out in full, but they should nevertheless, be understood as being repeated in full in each case. The symbol [ra] is used with the name of the Companions of the Holy Prophet[sa] and those of the Promised Messiah[as]. It stands for *Raḍī Allāhu ‘anhu/‘anhā/‘anhum* (May Allah be pleased with him/with her/with them). The symbol [rh] stands for *Raḥimahullāhu Ta‘ālā* (may Allah's blessings be on him). The symbol [aba] stands for *Ayyadahullāhu Ta‘ālā bi naṣrihil ‘azīz* (May Allah support him with His Mighty help).

The Publishers

GLOSSARY

‘Adal--The just.

Adhān--The formal call for Islāmic daily Prayers.

Ahl-e-Bait--The people of the household of the Holy Prophet of Islam[sa].

Aḥadīth--Plural of *hadith, See* Hadith.

Aḥmadī Muslim or an Aḥmadī--A member of the Aḥmadiyya Muslim Jamā‘at.

Aḥmadiyya Muslim Jamā‘at--(Also Aḥmadiyya) The Community of Muslims who accept the claims of Ḥaḍrat Mirzā Ghulām Aḥmad of Qādiān[as] as being the Promised Messiah and Mahdi; the Jamā‘at established by Ḥaḍrat Mirzā Ghulām Aḥmad[as] in 1889, now under the leadership of his fifth *Khalīfah,* Ḥaḍrat Mirzā Masroor Aḥmad[aba].

Allah--Allah is the personal name of God in Islam. To show proper reverence to Him, Muslims often add *Ta‘ālā,* 'the Most High', when saying His Holy name.

Al-Imam al-Mahdi--The title given to the Promised Reformer by the Holy Prophet Muḥammad[sa]; it means guided leader.

Amānah--Trust

Āmīn--May Allah make it so.

Bukhārī--A book of *aḥādīth* (the sayings) of the Holy Prophet Muḥammad[sa] compiled by Ḥaḍrat Imam Muḥammad Bin Ismā'īl Bukhārī[ra] (194H-256H). This book of *aḥādīth* is believed to be the most authentic book after the Holy Qur'an.

Dajjāl--A term in Arabic that literally means, 'the great deceiver.' In Islāmic terminology *'Dajjāl'* refers to those satanic forces that would be unleashed in the Latter Days to oppose the Promised Messiah and *al-Imam al-Mahdi.* A similar prophecy in the Christian faith about the appearance of the Antichrist refers to the same phenomenon, and we have therefore translated the term *'Dajjāl'* as 'Antichrist'.

Durūd or Durūd Sharīf--Invocation of blessings upon the Holy Prophet Muḥammad[sa].

Du'ā'--Prayer or supplication.

Hadith--A saying of the Holy Prophet Muḥammad[sa]. The plural is *aḥādīth.*

Ḥaḍrat--A term of respect used for a person of established righteousness and piety.

Ḥakam--The arbitrator.

Ḥalāl--Lawful, permissible or pure.

Ḥoly Prophet--A term used exclusively for Ḥaḍrat Muḥammad[sa], the Prophet of Islam.

Holy Qur'an--The Book sent by Allah for the guidance of mankind. It was revealed to the Holy Prophet Muḥammad[sa] over a period of twenty-three years.

Ḥuḍūr--Your Holiness; His Holiness.

Imam--The Arabic word for a leader. The head of the Aḥmadiyya Muslim Jamā'at is also referred to as the *Imam.*

Inshā'Allāh--An Arabic term meaning 'God-willing'.

'Īsā-- Jesus[as] son of Mary

Jamā'at-- Jamā'at means community. Although the word Jamā'at itself may refer to any community, in this book, Jamā'at specifically refers to the Aḥmadiyya Muslim Jamā'at.

Jihad-- Exerting oneself or striving.

Jizyah--A tax paid by non-Muslims living in a Muslim State in lieu of military service.

Ka'bah--House of Allah in Mecca.

Khalīfah--Caliph is derived from the Arabic word *Khalīfah,* which herein means the successor. *Khulafā'* is the plural of *Khalīfah.* Aḥmadī Muslims refer to each successor of the

Promised Messiah[as] as Khalīfatul Masīḥ.

Khalīfatul Masīḥ II--Ḥaḍrat Khalīfatul Masīḥ II, Mirzā Bashīr-ud-Dīn Maḥmūd Aḥmad[ra], was the second successor of the Promised Messiah[as]. He is also called Muṣleḥ-e-Mau'ūd (Promised Son) because he was born in accordance with the prophecy made by the Promised Messiah[as] in 1886 concerning the birth of a righteous son who would be endowed with unique abilities and attributes.

Khalīfatul Masīḥ IV--Ḥaḍrat Khalīfatul Masīḥ IV, Mirzā Ṭāhir Aḥmad[rh] (1928-2003), was the fourth successor of the Promised Messiah[as]. He was the grandson of the Founder of the Aḥmadiyya Muslim Jamā'at, Ḥaḍrat Mirzā Ghulām Aḥmad, the Promised Messiah[as].

Khalīfatul Masīḥ V--Ḥaḍrat Khalīfatul Masīḥ V, Mirzā Masroor Aḥmad[aba], is the fifth successor of the Promised Messiah[as] and the current Imam of Jamā'at-e-Aḥmadiyya. He is the great grandson of the Promised Messiah[as].

Khātamul Anbiyā'and Khātamun-Nabiyyīn--Seal of the Prophets.

Khilāfat--The institution of successorship in Islam.

Khulafā'--Plural of *Khalīfah, See* Khalīfah.

Mahdi--'The guided one'. This is the title given by the Holy Prophet Muḥammad[sa] to the awaited Reformer of the Latter Days.

Masīḥ-e-Mau'ūd--The Promised Messiah.

Maulāna or Maulavī--A Muslim religious cleric.

Momin--A true believer; a pious person.

Mo'edhdhin--A person who calls the *Adhān* (call to Prayer).

Muḥarram--The first month of the Islāmic Calendar.

Mujaddid-- Reformer.

Mullāh--A Muslim religious cleric.

Mūsā--Moses[as].

Nabī--Prophet.

Nuzūl--To descend.

(The) Promised Messiah--This term refers to the Founder of the Aḥmadiyya Muslim Jamā'at, Ḥaḍrat Mirza Ghulām Aḥmad of Qādiān[as]. He claimed that he had been sent by Allah in accordance with the prophecies of the Holy Prophet Muḥammad[sa] concerning the coming of *al-Imam al-Mahdi* and Messiah from among the Muslims.

Qamar--Moon of the night following the second night, and according to some it is the moon of the night following the third night.

Shahādah (Kalimah Shahādah)--The declaration of the Islāmic faith: to bear witness that there is none worthy of worship except Allah, He is One, without any associate, and to bear witness that the Holy Prophet Muḥammad is His servant and His Messenger; also known as the first pillar of Islam.

Sharia--Islāmic religious law.

Shirk--Associating partners with Allah.

Sīratun-Nabī Day--Tradition of holding conventions on the blessed life of the Holy Prophet[sa].

Sunnah--Traditions of the Holy Prophet Muḥammad of Islam[sa].

Sūrah--A term in Arabic referring to a chapter of the Holy Qur'an.

Tahajjud Prayer--Optional Prayer of great merit offered in the latter part of the night; pre-dawn formal Islamic worship.

Tauḥīd--The fundamental Islāmic belief that there is none worthy of being worshipped except Allah.

'Ulemā'--A class of Muslim scholars.

Ummah and Ummat-e-Muslimah--The larger community of Muslims; The Islamic community.

Umrah--Lesser Pilgrimage in which some of the rites of the Pilgrimage are left out.

FOREWORD

Since the beginning of mankind, a struggle has been going on between Truth and Falsehood, and between Light and Darkness. However, as it is the Way of Allah, Truth and Light always triumph. It has been the nature of certain people, that being arrogant, they challenge the Prophets of Allah to gain cheap fame. However, they always meet failure and humiliation. Many such people have adopted a brazen attitude towards the pride of the Universe, the Holy Prophet Muḥammad[sa]. All of them, as is the Way of Allah, failed miserably.

Recently, certain elements using freedom of conscious and freedom of speech as an excuse, have published foul caricatures in books and newspapers, either to show their malice towards Islam and the Holy Prophet[sa], or maybe, to spread hatred against Islam. As a result of this, there has been a violent reaction among various organizations and countries. They, in order to vent their anger and displeasure, have resorted to furious protests, often leading to arson and destruction of private and public property.

The main objective of establishing the Aḥmadiyya Muslim Jamā'at is, by the Grace of God, to spread the true teachings of Islam. Therefore, in such a provocative situation, the Jamā'at's reaction instead of setting up fires and causing damage and destruction of properties, always has been to give a satisfactory response to the criticism of the critics, and to make an effort to convey the true and real message of Islam to the World.

Accordingly, Ḥaḍrat Mirzā Masroor Aḥmad[aba], the Supreme Head of the Worldwide Aḥmadiyya Muslim Community, has thoroughly discussed the current events in his Friday Sermons of February 10, 17, 24, and March 3 and 10, 2006, which he delivered at Baitul Futūḥ Mosque, Morden, London. These Friday Sermons clearly spell out what should be the response of a true Muslim in such a precarious situation, and how one should tackle it effectively.

The members of the Aḥmadiyya Muslim Community should read these sermons and give these to their friends and acquaintances for reading, so that they also become familiar with the true teachings of Islam. For this purpose, these Friday Sermons will be translated, God willing, into different languages and published.

This English translation, which was rendered by Mrs. Shermīn Butt has been revised by myself and by Dr. Karīmullāh Zīrvī. Dr. Zīrvī has also worked very hard towards the setting of the book. May God Almighty grant the best reward to all the workers.

Munīr-ud-Dīn Shams
Additional Vakīlut-Taṣnīf
London
June 2006

Ḥaḍrat Mirzā Masroor Aḥmad
Khalīfatul Masīḥ V[aba]
Head of the worldwide Aḥmadiyya Muslim Community

THE AUTHOR

Ḥaḍrat Mirzā Masroor Aḥmad, Khalīfatul Masīḥ V[aba], is currently the supreme head of the worldwide Aḥmadiyyah Muslim Community. He is the fifth successor and great grandson of the Promised Messiah and Reformer, Ḥaḍrat Mirzā Ghulām Aḥmad[as] of Qādiān. He was elected to this position in London, England by an electoral college on April 22, 2003, a few days after the death of his predecessor, Ḥaḍrat Mirzā Ṭāhir Aḥmad, Khalīfatul Masīḥ IV[rta].

Ḥaḍrat Mirzā Masroor Aḥmad[aba] did his primary education at Ta'līm-ul-Islam High School Rabwah, and obtained his BA from Ta'līm-ul-Islam (TI) College Rabwah, Pakistan. In 1976 he earned his Masters of Science degree in Agricultural Economics from the Agriculture University Faisalabad, Pakistan.

Prior to his being elected as Khalīfah, Ḥaḍrat Mirzā Masroor Aḥmad[aba] accumulated an impressive record of humanitarian services that underscore his commitment to education and philanthropy. His altruistic endeavours took him to Ghana in 1977 where, for several years, he served as a principal of various Aḥmadiyyah Muslim schools. He helped to inaugurate the Aḥmadiyyah Secondary School Salaga, where he served as principal for the school's first two years.

Ḥaḍrat Mirzā Masroor Aḥmad[aba] was able to make use of the knowledge of his studied discipline, agricultural economics, to carry out research about wheat production in

Ghana. The first successful experiment of planting, growing and nurturing wheat as an economic crop in Ghana was exhibited at an international trade fair and the results were submitted to the Ministry of Agriculture of Ghana.

In December of 1997, Ḥaḍrat Mirzā Masroor Aḥmad[aba] was appointed to the office of Nāẓir-e-A'lā (chief executive director) of the Ṣadr Anjuman Aḥmadiyyah Pakistan. In 1999, Ḥaḍrat Mirzā Masroor Aḥmad[aba] was falsely charged with blasphemy and wrongly accused of defaming verses of the Holy Qur'an. He was arrested and imprisoned for eleven days in his hometown of Rabwah until it was shown that the charges brought against him were entirely unfounded.

Ḥaḍrat Mirzā Masroor Aḥmad[aba] currently resides in London, England. As spiritual leader of Aḥmadī Muslims all over the world, he vigorously champions the cause of Islam through a refreshing message of peace and compassion.

(1)

Friday Sermon delivered on 10th February, 2006 at Baitul Futūh Mosque, Morden, London, UK

****

(1)

Friday Sermon delivered on 10th February, 2006

- We should tell the world about the character of the Excellent Exampler, the Holy Prophet[sa], particularly, with regard to his mercy and love for humanity. We should enlighten the public, in each country, about the noble character of the Holy Prophet[sa], and we should try to become righteous.

- We strongly condemn publication of the extremely contemptible, provocative, and blasphemous caricatures of the Holy Prophet[sa]. Aḥmadiyya Muslim Jamā'at's reaction to the incident while remaining within the Islamic teachings and its positive results.

- This shows how much they detest Muslims and Islam and how much malice they have for Islam. Their obnoxious minds show how far away they have gone from God Almighty.

- Burning of flags, creating turmoil, or going on

strike is not a good way to protest.

- We should mould our attitude according to the Islamic values and teachings. Our response always should be such, which elegantly reflects the excellent personality and character of the Holy Prophet[sa].

- Aḥmadīs should study and enter the field of Journalism.

****

اَشْهَدُ اَنْ لَّا اِلٰهَ اِلَّا اللّٰهُ وَحْدَهُ لَا شَرِيْكَ لَهُ، وَ اَشْهَدُ اَنَّ مُحَمَّدًا عَبْدُهُ وَرَسُوْلُهُ.

اَمَّا بَعْدُ فَاَعُوْذُ بِاللّٰهِ مِنَ الشَّيْطٰنِ الرَّجِيْمِ

بِسْمِ اللّٰهِ الرَّحْمٰنِ الرَّحِيْمِ ٠

اَلْحَمْدُ لِلّٰهِ رَبِّ الْعٰلَمِيْنَ ٠ الرَّحْمٰنِ الرَّحِيْمِ ٠ مٰلِكِ يَوْمِ الدِّيْنِ ٠ اِيَّاكَ نَعْبُدُ وَاِيَّاكَ نَسْتَعِيْنُ ٠ اِهْدِنَا الصِّرَاطَ الْمُسْتَقِيْمَ ٠ صِرَاطَ الَّذِيْنَ اَنْعَمْتَ عَلَيْهِمْ ۙ غَيْرِ الْمَغْضُوْبِ عَلَيْهِمْ وَلَا الضَّآلِّيْنَ ٠

وَمَآ اَرْسَلْنٰكَ اِلَّا رَحْمَةً لِّلْعٰلَمِيْنَ ٠

اِنَّ اللّٰهَ وَمَلٰٓئِكَتَهُ، يُصَلُّوْنَ عَلَى النَّبِيِّ ؕ يٰٓاَيُّهَا الَّذِيْنَ اٰمَنُوْا صَلُّوْا عَلَيْهِ وَسَلِّمُوْا تَسْلِيْمًا ٠ اِنَّ الَّذِيْنَ يُؤْذُوْنَ اللّٰهَ وَرَسُوْلَهُ، لَعَنَهُمُ اللّٰهُ فِى الدُّنْيَا وَالْاٰخِرَةِ وَاَعَدَّ لَهُمْ عَذَابًا مُّهِيْنًا ٠

I bear witness that there is none worthy of worship except Allah, He is One and has no partner. And I bear witness that Muḥammad is His Servant and Messenger.

After this, I seek refuge with Allah from Satan, the rejected

In the Name of Allah, the Gracious, the Merciful

All praise belongs to Allah, Lord of all the worlds. The Gracious, the Merciful. Master of the Day of Judgment. Thee alone do we worship and Thee alone do we implore for help. Guide us in the right path -- The path of those on whom Thou has bestowed *Thy* blessings, those who have not incurred displeasure, and those who have not gone astray. (Sūrah Al-Fātihah, 1:1-7)

And We have sent thee not but as a mercy for all peoples. (Sūrah al-Anbiyā', 21:108)

Allah and His angels send blessings on the Prophet. O ye who believe! you *also* should invoke blessings on him and salute *him* with the salutation of peace. Verily, those who malign Allah and His Messengers - Allah has cursed them in this world and in the Hereafter, and has prepared for them an abasing punishment. (Sūrah Al-Aḥzāb, 33:57-58)

Reaction of the Muslim world to the publication of the most obnoxious caricatures in Denmark and other Western countries.

Recently, newspapers in Denmark and some Western countries have published extremely foul and provocative caricatures with reference to the Holy Prophet[sa] that are inflammatory to the sentiments of Muslims. Due to this, a wave of indignation is running across the Muslim world. Each Muslim is reacting to this. Anyway, there had to be an expression of the inherent reaction to such an act. Clearly, for an Aḥmadī, who is certainly at the forefront in his love and devotion for the Holy Prophet[sa], due to the Promised Messiah[as], whose perception and comprehension of the Seal of the Prophets[sa] is far greater than that of others. Many Aḥmadīs are writing letters and expressing their indignation. They give suggestions that there should be a constant effort to impart to the world the station of this great Prophet[sa]. Wherever the Community is active, work is being carried out on this. However, as we know we do not ever react by going on strikes or by setting fires; nor is setting fires, strikes, damage and destruction or burning flags the solution for this.

In this day and age, religious people from other religions as well as the Western world are attacking Islam and the Founder of Islam[sa]. Currently, the West has no interest in religion. The majority of them are lost in the amusements of this world and are involved in this to such an extent that no matter what their religion is, Islam or Christianity or any other religion, they have no care for it and have totally abandoned it. The majority have lost any sense of sanctity for religion; in fact, there was news, probably from France, the other day, that if we so wish, God forbid, we can even caricature God. This is their condition. So at this most disgraceful act of the cartoonist, and their thinking that goes with it, many commentators have written about the reaction emerging from the Muslim world. They claim that this reaction is a clash between the Islamic world and the Western secular democracy, although it has nothing to do with society. As I said earlier, their majority has lost all sense of morals; immorality is espoused in the name of freedom, and modesty has all but vanished.

Comments made by certain fair-minded observers

Anyhow, even on this occasion, there are some decent and fair-minded writers among them who have stated that it is wrong to call this reaction a clash between Islam and Western secular democracy. Robert Fisk, a columnist from England, has written adopting a very fair approach. Someone from Denmark had written that this is a clash between Islamic society and Western secular democracy, on this he [R. Fisk] wrote that this is totally incorrect; this is not a clash of civilisations or secularism. He writes that this is not even a freedom of speech issue. It is just that for the Muslims, the Prophet[sa] received Divine words directly from God, in that he was God's spokesperson on the earth. Whereas they (Christians) consider (this is a Christian writing) that Prophets and Saints have been lost in the haze of history due to their teachings not being in concordance with the modern-day concept of human rights and freedom. Muslims consider religion a part of their everyday life and despite the passing centuries, and their ensuing alterations, they still maintain this thought. Whereas we have practically separated religion from everyday life. For this reason, we do not talk about Christianity versus Islam. Instead, we talk about Western civilization versus Islam. On this basis we are also inclined to think that if we can make fun of our Prophets or their teachings, then why not of other religions?

He also questions if this attitude (by the Muslims) is all that impulsive anyway? He writes that he remembers a decade ago a film entitled, 'Last Temptation of Christ', was released, which raised a lot of protest and condemnation because it depicted Ḥaḍrat 'Īsā[as] with a woman in an objectionable way. A cinema was burnt down in Paris in anger, and a young French man was murdered. What is this supposed to mean? On one hand, there are some among us who cannot tolerate defamation of religious sentiments; however, we also expect Muslims to tolerate publication of caricatures made in bad taste in the name of freedom of expression. Is this the right attitude? The Western leaders make me laugh by maintaining that they cannot put restrictions on newspapers and freedom of expression. He writes that if the controversial caricatures were to depict the turban-shaped bomb on the head of some Jewish Rabbi, rather than the Prophet of Islam[sa], would it not have raised a protest on the lines that it smacked of anti-Semitism and that it was hurtful to the Jews? If it is a matter of upholding freedom of speech why then is 'Holocaust denial' a crime in France, Germany and Austria? Few would have raised an objection if these caricatures would have encouraged those who support religious reformation or fair-mindedness among Muslims and wish to promote enlightened discussions. However, what other message have the caricatures conveyed than that Islam is a militant religion. Apart from spreading incitement and agitation all round, what positive steps have these caricatures produced?

(Daily *'Jang'*, London 7th February, 2006, pp. 1-3)

Anyhow, the likelihood of this action also came about somewhat due to the attitude of Muslims. However, there are decent people among them (the Westerners) who like to state the facts.

Improper reaction by certain Muslim leaders provides an opportunity for the opponents to defame Islam

I have had reports about the reactions from different countries; reactions by Muslims as well as the viewpoints of governmental officials of European countries, or those of journalists. There are a substantial number of people among these who have disapproved of the step taken by the newspaper. Yet, as I said, somewhere or the other, at times, such mischief is let loose that makes the filth of their minds and remoteness from God evident, and demonstrates their prejudice and malice against Islam. However, I would say that it is unfortunate that due to the erroneous reaction of certain Muslim leaders, these people get a chance to disgrace Islam. It is these very matters that are later used for political gains. The attitude of Muslims, in their daily life, can be such that it irritates these governments, for example, their tendency to stay out of work; mostly these people sit at home and seek social security or carry out jobs that evade tax and many other such things. Muslims themselves provide the opportunity from which these alert nations take advantage.

At times, it is these people who are the perpetrators, but due to the wrong reaction of the Muslims, they appear to be the victims and the Muslims are deemed the villains. It is correct that a large majority of Muslims does not approve of the damage and destruction. Yet it is the leadership or a few roguish elements that brings the notoriety. For instance, in a report from Denmark into the aftermath of the issue, the response of the Danish people is that Muslims should accept the apology of the newspaper. They want to end this problem in a peaceful manner so that the real teachings of Islam reach them, and violence can be avoided. Television is reporting that, having watched the reaction against their country, the burning of their national flag and embassies being set alight, Danish children are anxious and frightened. They feel in danger of a war looming with threats made to their lives. As a result, the public and some politicians have disapproved of this and an emerging opinion is that of having a large mosque built for the Muslims to recompense for their hurt sentiments. This would be funded by Danish companies and the supreme Mayor of Copenhagen has favoured the suggestion. As I said, the great majority of Muslims also opines that we should accept the apology. However, one of their (Muslims) leaders who represents 27 organisations, is reported to have said that although the newspaper has apologised they should do so once again face to face. It is then that they would take the message to the Muslim countries to stop the campaign. They try and depict Islam in a most horrific manner. Rather than be forthcoming in reconciliation they are inclined towards hostility. Although the Aḥmadiyya Muslim Community has nothing to do with these disorderly situations yet our missions also receive threatening phone calls and letters from certain opponents. May Allah keep all our mosques and missions safe and protect them from their harm.

In any case, an erroneous reaction gives way to an erroneous proclamation. As I said once, the apology of these people for their actions is viewed against the reaction of the Muslims; then despite being the perpetrators, for they perpetrated an extremely wrong act, they become the victims. They are apologising in Denmark, but the Muslim leaders are adamant. These Muslims should employ some wisdom, and should have some sense, and change their reactionary ways.

The way an Aḥmadī should react

As I said, possibly, rather certainly, our hearts are the most aggrieved at this act. However, our mode of response is different. I would mention here that it will not be far-fetched, that as before, they will continue to make similar mischief time to time; that is, they will do something or the other that would again cause hurt to Muslims. Another objective behind this could be to use this as an excuse to put legal restrictions on Muslims, in particular those who have emigrated from the East, from the Indian sub-continent. Anyhow, despite the fact whether they put restrictions or not, we should formulate our responses according to the Islamic values and teachings.

As I said, from the very beginning these conspiracies have been carried out against Islam and the Holy Prophet[sa]. However, as it is Allah's promise to safeguard Islam, therefore, He has been protecting it, and all the opposing efforts are met with failure.

The Promised Messiah[as] came to defend Islam and the Holy Prophet[sa] against conspiracies

For this age, Allah appointed the Promised Messiah[as] to fulfil this objective. With regard to the attacks made on the blessed person of the Holy Prophet[sa], in this age, the Promised Messiah[as], himself, and later on by following his teachings, his *Khulafā'*, guided the Community and demonstrated responses that bore [positive] consequences. I shall present a couple of examples of this so that the achievements of the Community are made clear to those who allege that by not participating in the boycotts and by not joining them Aḥmadīs demonstrate that we feel no pain over the defamation of the Holy Prophet[sa].

Our response always is, and always should be, one that is lucid in conveying the blessed model and teachings of the Holy Prophet[sa]; and lucid in, as well, presenting the teachings of the Holy Qur'an. Rather than be involved in subversive activities when faced with attacks on the blessed person of the Holy Prophet[sa], we turn to Allah and seek His help. I shall now present two examples, which show the honour of the love of the Holy Prophet[sa] of his true and ardent devotee, the Promised Messiah[as].

The first example is that of 'Abdullāh Ātham, who was a Christian and had revealed his extremely depraved mind by using the word *Dajjāl*, God forbid, for the Holy Prophet[sa] in his book. At that time, a discussion was underway with the Promised Messiah[as] about Islam and Christianity. A debate was ongoing.

The Promised Messiah[as] states:

> Thus, I was engaged in debate for fifteen days, the discussion continued and I privately continued to pray for Ātham's chastisement; that is, for punishment for the words he had used. When the discussion was over I said to him that one debate has ended but a contest of one sort remains, which is from God and is that you have termed our Prophet[sa] with the name *Dajjāl* in your book *'Andrūna Bible'.* I deem the Prophet[sa] to be truthful and honest and believe the religion of Islam to be from Allah. Thus, this is the contest that shall be settled by the heavenly decision, and the heavenly decision is that whoever among the two of us is a liar and unfairly terms the Prophet[sa] as a liar and *Dajjāl* and is an enemy of the Truth, shall, during the lifetime of the person who is truthful, be doomed to nether hell within fifteen months from this day onwards; unless he turns to the Truth. That is, desists from calling the truthful and honest Prophet[sa], *Dajjāl* and abandons impudence and foul language. It is thus said because simply denying a religion does not determine punishment in this world. Rather, it is brazenness, impudence, and foul language that determines punishment.

The Promised Messiah[as] further states:

> When I said these words his face turned pale, he was ashen

and his hands began to tremble. He then promptly stuck his tongue out, put his hands to his ears and started shaking his head and his hands in the manner that a frightened criminal vehemently pleads not guilty and comes across most repentant and humble. He kept uttering, again and again, that he had not been disrespectful and impudent, and he did not ever speak against Islam again.

So this was the response of the gallant of God who had a great sense of honour for the Holy Prophet[sa] and who would challenge those who committed acts like these.

Then there was a person called Lekh Rām, who used abusive language for the Holy Prophet[sa]. The Promised Messiah[as] tried to stop him from this impertinence. He did not desist. Eventually the Promised Messiah[as] prayed and Allah revealed to him the news of the man's painful death.

The Promised Messiah[as] says that:

> Allah the Exalted has given me a pledge about the enemy of God and the Prophet[sa], who uses foul and vulgar language for the Holy Prophet[sa] and is called Lekh Rām. Allah the Exalted has accepted my prayer and in answer to my malediction for him, gave me the tidings that he shall die within six years. This is a sign for those who seek the true religion. This is exactly what happened and he died a most painful death.

Enlighten the excellences of the Holy Prophet's[sa] personality and chracter to the world

These are the ways the Promised Messiah[as] has taught us; to counsel those who act improperly, to relate the virtues of the Holy Prophet[sa], to make the world aware of these beautiful and luminous aspects that are unknown to the world. Pray to Allah that He keeps them away from these improprieties or that He chastises them. Allah has His own ways of chastisement, and He knows best how to chastise whom.

Later, in the time of the second Khilāfat, a vulgar book entitled *'Rangīla Rasūl'* came out, and a magazine, *Wartamān* published a vulgar article which aroused the Muslims of India. There was great incitement among Muslims all over, and they reacted most strongly.

Addressing the Muslims at this occasion, Ḥaḍrat Muṣleḥ-e-Mau'ūd, Khalīfatul Masīh II[ra] said:

> O brothers! I say with heart-felt compassion one more time that one who starts fighting is not brave. He is a coward because he has been overcome by his 'self'. According to a Hadith, the one who suppresses anger is truly brave. It is said that the brave is one who makes a resolute determination and then does not waver from it until he accomplishes it. He said, 'Make a pledge for three things for the progress of Islam; first of all you will have fear of God and will not be flippant about religion. So,

firstly reform yourself. Secondly, be fully interested in conveying the message of Islam. The teachings of Islam should reach each person in the world. The qualities of the Holy Prophet[sa], the virtues of his beautiful life, his blessed model should be known. Thirdly, you should fully try to save the Muslims from social and economical subjugation.

(Anwārul 'Ulūm, Vol. 9, PP. 555-556)

This is now the obligation of each Muslim, the ordinary person as well as the leaders. You will find that despite having independence, the Muslim countries that are known as independent are subject to social and economic subjugation. They are at the mercy of the Western countries and are inclined towards imitating them. Rather than work themselves, they mostly rely on them. It is for this reason that time and time again, they play with the sentiments of Muslims. He also initiated the tradition of holding conventions on the blessed life of the Holy Prophet[sa]. These are the ways of showing disapproval, rather than sabotage and disorder. While addressing the Muslims he predominantly spoke to the Aḥmadīs about these points.

Some wrong traditions of these countries are imperceptibly creeping into some of our families. I say to Aḥmadīs that you too were addressed therein. Do adopt what is good in their culture, but we should avoid what is wrong. Our reaction should be this, rather than damage and destruction. Our attention should be drawn towards self-reflection, to analyse what our deeds are, how much fear of God do we have, how much attention do we pay towards

His worship, how much attention do we pay to abide by religious commandments, and how much attention do we pay to deliver the message of Allah the Exalted to others!

Later, in the era of the fourth Khilāfat, [Salmān] Rushdī wrote a most offensive book. At that time, Ḥaḍrat Khalīfatul Masīḥ IV[rh] delivered sermons concerning it and had someone write a book about it. Then, as I said, these improprieties are ongoing. In the beginning of last year, a similar article came out on the life of the Holy Prophet[sa]. At that time I drew attention of the Community, as well as of the auxiliary organizations to write articles and letters and to widen communications; to cite the virtues and attributes of the Holy Prophet[sa]. This is a matter that requires presenting the beautiful aspects of the life of the Holy Prophet[sa] to the world and this cannot be achieved by damage and destruction. For this reason, Aḥmadīs of all social backgrounds in all countries should also include other educated and sensible Muslims in presenting a peaceful reaction by widening communications and writing. In this way, reason would be accomplished in each country and each social sphere, and after this, if anyone still takes a step then their matter is with God.

Allah the Exalted sent the Holy Prophet[sa] as a mercy for the whole of mankind as He Himself states:

وَمَآ اَرْسَلْنٰكَ اِلَّا رَحْمَةً لِّلْعٰلَمِيْنَ 0

And We have sent thee not but as a mercy for all peoples. (Sūrah Al-Anbiyā', 21:108)

A being as great as him, one who dispensed mercy, [the like of him] neither existed before nor could come later. Indeed his blessed model shall remain forever, and each Muslim should try to follow it. For this the greatest responsibility lies on an Aḥmadī; it befalls upon us. In any case, the Holy Prophet[sa] was a mercy for all peoples. While these people depict him in a manner that portrays a most horrific concept. We have to tell the world about the blessed loving and compassionate model of the Holy Prophet[sa]. It is obvious that to do this, the Muslims will also have to changetheir attitudes. There could be absolutely no issue of terrorism or militancy, the Holy Prophet[sa] would always try to avoid war, until the time when he came to Medīna, and war was imposed on him. Then with Allah's permission, war had to be fought in defence. However, there was also the commandment of Allah:

وَ قَاتِلُوْا فِيْ سَبِيْلِ اللّٰهِ الَّذِيْنَ يُقَاتِلُوْنَكُمْ وَلَا تَعْتَدُوْا ط اِنَّ
اللّٰهَ لَا يُحِبُّ الْمُعْتَدِيْنَ 0

And fight in the cause of Allah against those who fight you, but do not transgress. Surely, Allah loves not the transgressors. (Sūrah Al-Baqarah, 2:191)

Certainly the Holy Prophet[sa] was the greatest of all adherents of the *Sharia* that was revealed to him. It is extremely cruel to convey such disgraceful thoughts about him. Anyhow, as it is being said that they have apologised, and our missionary has also reported that one of them apologised; had expressed regret.

The immediate response of the Aḥmadiyya Muslim Community at the publication of the caricatures

The other Muslims are incited to strike actions, damage and destruction and such is their response. The Aḥmadiyya Muslim Community promptly reacted to this in the manner they should have. The Aḥmadīs promptly communicated with the newspapers. This is not a matter that took place today that they are taking strike actions in February 2006. This incident took place last year in September. When the mischief was made how did we respond? As I said, this took place in September or maybe early October, and our Missionary promptly prepared a detailed article which was sent to the newspaper that had published the caricature; a protest was made at this publication. The teaching of the Promised Messiah[as] was explained and they were told that this is our way of protest. We will not launch a rally but we will do the Jihad of the pen with you and express our feelings of sadness at the publication of the images. They were told that freedom of conscience notwithstanding, it is not meant to hurt the sentiment of others. Anyway, this was met with a positive response. An article was sent to the newspaper which was published. Danish people responded very well to it. As our Mission House received telephone calls and letters with messages of appreciation about the article. Moreover, the President of the Journalists' Union extended an invitation to a meeting. There it was explained to them that although the law allowed for freedom of conscience, it did not mean that others' religious leaders and revered persons should be demeaned. It was crucial to look after the feelings of the Muslims and the Christians as they co-existed in the society because there could be no peace without this.

They were also told of the beautiful teachings of the Holy Prophet[sa], his excellent model, his high morals and civility, his compassion for people and for the creation of God, and that he was the personification of compassion and affection. A few incidents were related to them and the question was raised that how such images could be made about a person whose teaching was such and whose deeds were such? They greatly appreciated our Missionary's input. One cartoonist openly said that had such a meeting taken place beforehand he would have never made the caricature. Now he knows the teaching of Islam. Everyone agreed that dialogue should continue.

The President of the Union issued a press release; its text was read out to all. A television interview took place which went well; a meeting with a Minister also took place. Anyway, the Community continues to endeavour; similar actions have been taken in other countries, and, in any case, a lot of work was done where the issue started. The basis for the creation of these caricatures is a book by a Danish writer entitle, 'The life of the Prophet and Qur'an', which is on sale now. The author of this book had asked the public to send pictures of the Holy Prophet[sa], some were sent anonymously lest there was a Muslim reaction. So the reason for this incident seems to be the book. However, in the case of the newspaper, the basis were also the caricatures. They should also make constant efforts in this regard and everywhere in the world as well; if it [the book] is read and anything objectionable is found, the matter should be addressed and answers should be given [to any questions raised]. There is also a perception in Denmark that certain Muslims are showing different caricatures than the ones published to incite the Muslim world. It is not known whether this is true or not, however, with our prompt attention they have developed some awareness. This action was taken immediately, while these people have come to know now, even though this happened three months ago.

As I said, there is a need to present and promote the aspects of the blessed life of the Holy Prophet[sa] in each country. In particular, it is our obligation to dismiss the misconception about Islam being militant with reasoning and argument. I have advised before to write to newspapers in abundance. Writers and newspapers could also be sent books on the blessed life of the Holy Prophet[sa].

Aḥmadī youth should enter the field of Journalism

Another suggestion is that the Community should plan for the future in that young people should try to go into journalism as much as possible; those who are more inclined this way, so that we may have our influence in newspapers and such places. For this kind of mischief is going to continue to emerge from time to time. If the maximum links can be made with the media these matters can be stopped, these vulgarities can be stopped. If after all this, someone is still obstinate, they would come under the category of those upon whom is Allah's curse in this world and the Hereafter. God Almighty states:

إِنَّ الَّذِيْنَ يُؤْذُوْنَ اللّٰهَ وَرَسُوْلَهٗ لَعَنَهُمُ اللّٰهُ فِى الدُّنْيَا
وَالْاٰخِرَةِ وَاَعَدَّ لَهُمْ عَذَابًا مُّهِيْنًا 0

Verily, those who annoy Allah and His Messengers - Allah has cursed them in this world and in the Heareafter, and has prepared for them an abasing punishment. (Sūrah Al-Aḥzāb, 33:58)

This commandment has not ceased, our Prophet[sa] is a living Prophet, his teaching is eternally life-infusing, his *Sharia* is one that can solve problems of all time and era, and following him grants nearness to Allah. For these reasons, the hurt and pain that is inflicted on those who believe in him remains true to this day in each and every way. Allah is a Living God and He is watching over their misdeeds.

It is our obligation to inform the world. We will have to communicate to the world that Allah the Exalted has the power, even today, to punish the pain and torment you inflict. Therefore, desist from hurting Allah and His Prophet[sa]. However, while we have to impart the teachings of Islam and the blessed model of the Holy Prophet[sa] to the world, we also need to reform our deeds. It will be our deeds alone that shall silence the world and will play the most significant role in silencing the world. As I mentioned in the report, duplicity is being alleged against a Muslim scholar, in that he says one thing here and goes there and does the opposite [incites people]. Maybe, I did not read that report. So we need to present practical models of our outer-self and our inner-self, corresponding with each other, and also harmonization in our words and deeds.

Flag burning or demolition will not establish the honour of the Holy Prophet[sa]

I also say this to those who are known as Muslims, any whether or not they are Aḥmadīs, Shias or Sunnīs or belong to any other sects of Islam; when the person of the Holy Prophet[sa] is attacked, rather than exhibiting momentary passion, burning flags, causing damage and destruction and attacking embassies, reform their deeds instead, so that the others do not get a chance to point their finger at them. Do they believe that setting fires, God forbid, is all that demonstrates the honour and station of the Holy Prophet[sa], and by burning flags or burning the property of an embassy they have had their reprisal? No! We are followers of the Holy Prophet[sa], who came to put the fire out, who was the Ambassador of Love, was the Prince of Peace. So rather than take harsh actions, impart his beautiful teaching to the World.

May Allah give the Muslims sense and understanding. However, I say to the Aḥmadīs that these people do not know and who knows if they will come to their senses or not? In response to the publication of the offensive caricatures, each child, each elderly, each youth, each man and each woman among you should kindle a fire that would never extinguish. Not a fire to burn down the flag or property of a country that extinguishes in a few minutes or a few hours. Here they stand showing great enthusiasm (in a photograph from Pakistan) in setting fires, as if they have had a great achievement - this fire would extinguish in five minutes! The fire we light should be such that would blaze forever and that is the fire of love and devotion for the Holy Prophet[sa], the fire to adopt each of his blessed models and demonstrate it to the world. Once this is inflamed in your hearts, it shall keep burning. This fire should be such that it would also be moulded in prayers with its flames ever reaching the heavens!

Turn your anguish into prayers and invoke blessings upon the Holy Prophet[sa], in abundance

This is the fire that every Aḥmadī has to kindle in their hearts and have to mould their pains into prayers. Yet, for all this, the mediator has to be the Holy Prophet[sa]. For the acceptance of our prayers, to attract the love of God, to avoid the absurdities of the world, to protect ourselves from wickedness of this kind that take place, to keep the love of the Holy Prophet[sa] alive in our hearts, for the good of our life in this world and the Hereafter, we should invoke blessings and salutations on the Holy Prophet[sa], immeasurably. Indeed we should do so profusely. In this seditious time, to keep ourselves immeresed in the love of the Holy Prophet[sa] and to keep our next generations firm on Aḥmadiyyat and Islam, each Aḥmadī should strictly adhere to the commandment that:

إِنَّ اللّٰهَ وَمَلٰٓئِكَتَهٗ يُصَلُّوْنَ عَلَى النَّبِيِّ ط يٰٓاَيُّهَا الَّذِيْنَ اٰمَنُوْا
صَلُّوْا عَلَيْهِ وَسَلِّمُوْا تَسْلِيْمًا 0

Allah and His angels send blessings on the Prophet. O ye who believe! you *also* should invoke blessings on him and salute *him* with the salutation of peace.

(Sūrah Al-Aḥzāb, 33:57)

The Holy Prophet[sa] once said, in fact there are many references of this, that for me the blessings of Allah and His angels is sufficient, the commandment for you is for your own protection.

(1. Tafsīr Durr-e-Manthūr, Targhīb-e-Asfahānī. 2. Musnad Dailamī ba-ḥawạlah 'Durūd Sharīf', Compiled by Maulānā Muḥammad Ismā'īl Ḥalālpurī, New Edition)

We are, therefore, in need of invoking these blessings for the acceptance of our prayers. On balance, this verse and the first section of this Hadith gives the assurance that no matter how much they try to deride or disparage the station of the Holy Prophet[sa] they can never succeed against the prayers of blessings and salutations that Allah and His angels are invoking on him. They can never gain anything from the attacks they make on the most blessed person of the Holy Prophet[sa] and, God willing, Islam is going to progress and triumph in the world and the banner of the Holy Prophet[sa] shall be raised all over the world.

As I said, in this age, Allah the Exalted has destined this through his true and ardent devotee, the Promised Messiah[sa].

There is a reference of Ḥaḍrat Maulāna 'Abdul Karīm Siālkotī[ra], he says in an extract:

> Once I heard from Ḥaḍrat Imam[as] that Allah had given him these stations by virtue of his invoking blessings on the Holy Prophet[sa]. He said, 'I see the beneficences of Allah reach the Holy Prophet[sa] in a most wondrous luminous form, and they are absorbed in the breast of the Holy Prophet[sa] from, there, they emerge through innumerable tubes which reach each rightful person in proportion to the worth of their share. Certainly no beneficence can reach others without the means of the Holy Prophet[sa].

He then said:

> What is *Durūd Sharīf* – to call upon that lofty station of the Holy Prophet[sa], through which these tubes of spiritual light

emerge. It is incumbent upon whoever wishes to have the blessings and beneficence of Allah the Exalted to invoke *Durūd Sharīf* in abundance so that the beneficence is stirred.

(Al-Ḥakam, Vol. 7, No. 8, p. 7, 28th February, 1903)

May Allah make it so that to avoid the evils of the world and to foster the love of the Holy Prophet[sa] in our hearts, to spread his teachings in the world, and we continue to be the recipients of the blessing and beneficence by invoking *Durūd*, by turning to Allah and seeking His help. May God Almighty help us.

(2)

Friday Sermon Delivered on 17th February, 2006 at Baitul Futūh Mosque, Morden, London, UK

****

(2)

Friday Sermon Delivered on 17th February, 2006

- Persistent activities intended to blaspheme the Holy Prophet[sa] will incite the Wrath of God Almighty.

- These earthquakes, hurricanes, and other calamities are not specifically for Asia only. The Promised Messiah[as] of God Almighty has warned Europe and America also. Therefore, they should fear Allah and should not challenge the Honour of God Almighty.

- God Almighty Who cares very much for His Honour and His beloved's honour can manifest His Might and Grandeur.

- Muslim countries and Muslims should correct their attitude. They should enlighten the world on the high status and excellent manners of the Holy Prophet[sa].

- Today, God Almighty has sent the true follower and ardent devotee of the Holy Prophet[sa] to guidethe Muslims, rather the whole world, towards right path. They must accept him and follow him.

- The Jamā'at of the Promised Messiah[as] will establish the glory of Islam and sanctity of the Holy Prophet[sa], God Willing.

- Aḥmadīs should openly explain to the followers of all religions that the awaited saviour, according to their teachings and expectations, has come.

****

اَشْهَدُ اَنْ لَّآ اِلٰهَ اِلَّا اللّٰهُ وَحْدَهٗ لَا شَرِيْكَ لَهٗ وَ اَشْهَدُ اَنَّ
مُحَمَّدًا عَبْدُهٗ وَرَسُوْلُهٗ .

اَمَّا بَعْدُ فَاَعُوْذُ بِاللّٰهِ مِنَ الشَّيْطٰنِ الرَّجِيْمِ

بِسْمِ اللّٰهِ الرَّحْمٰنِ الرَّحِيْمِ 0

اَلْحَمْدُ لِلّٰهِ رَبِّ الْعٰلَمِيْنَ 0 الرَّحْمٰنِ الرَّحِيْمِ 0 مٰلِكِ
يَوْمِ الدِّيْنِ 0 اِيَّاكَ نَعْبُدُ وَاِيَّاكَ نَسْتَعِيْنُ 0 اِهْدِنَا
الصِّرَاطَ الْمُسْتَقِيْمَ 0 صِرَاطَ الَّذِيْنَ اَنْعَمْتَ عَلَيْهِمْ ەۙ
غَيْرِ الْمَغْضُوْبِ عَلَيْهِمْ وَلَا الضَّآلِّيْنَ 0

I bear witness that there is none worthy of worship except Allāh, He is One and has no partner. And I bear witness that Muḥammad is His Servant and Messenger.

After this, I seek refuge with Allah from Satan, the rejected

In the Name of Allah, the Gracious, the Merciful

All praise belongs to Allah, Lord of all the worlds. The Gracious, the Merciful. Master of the Day of Judgment. Thee alone do we worship and Thee alone do we implore for help. Guide us in the right path---The path of those on whom Thou has bestowed *Thy* blessings, those who have not incurred displeasure, and those who have not gone astray. (Sūrah Al-Fātiḥah, 1:1-7)

I had meant to continue, in the last Friday Sermon, the subject of the previous two sermons. However, in light of the disgraceful and vulgar action of some Western newspapers, which sent shockwaves of indignation throughout the Muslim world, and the ensuing reaction, I felt it necessary to speak concerning it. This was so that Aḥmadīs could also be informed as to what our attitudes should be in such circumstances. Although, by the Grace of God, they do know this, but a reminder is needed that the world may also know the correct way for a Muslim to respond in these circumstances.

Injuring the sentiments of others is neither democracy, nor freedom of conscience

We tell the world that any kind of vulgar expression about any sacred person of any religion does not constitute freedom in any way at all. You apparently champion democracy and freedom of expression, but play with the sentiments of others; this is neither democracy nor freedom of expression. Everything has a limit and some code of conduct. Just as there are codes of conduct in all professions, there is also a code of conduct in journalism. Just as no matter what kind of government there is, it has its rules and regulations. Freedom of expression certainly does not mean that sentiments are trifled with, or are caused to be hurt. If this is the freedom that the West is proud of, then this freedom does not lead to advancement, rather it leads to decline.

Persistent activities intended to blaspheme the Holy Prophet[sa] will incite the Wrath of God Almighty

The West is swiftly abandoning religion and is demolishing moral values in every field in the name of freedom. They are oblivious to how they are inviting their own destruction. Recently, an Italian Minister has started a new mischief in printing these offensive caricatures on T-shirts, and wearing it. He has invited others to get these from him. It is said that these are also being sold. They say this is what the Muslims deserve. These people should understand that we do not know whether the Muslims deserve this or not. However, through these improprieties, they are certainly incurring the Wrath of God. Whatever happened in foolishness, happened. However, to prolong it with obstinacy and to insist that whatever they are doing is right is what definitely incurs the Wrath of God.

How Aḥmadīs should react under such circumstances

Anyhow, as I said the reaction of the rest of the Muslims is up to them. However, the response of an Aḥmadī Muslim should be to make them understand and to warn them about the Wrath of God. As I have said before, present the beautiful picture of the Holy Prophet[sa] to the world, turn to the All Powerful God and seek His help. If these people are heading towards destruction, then God, Who has His own sense of honour, and a sense of honour for His dear ones, has the power to manifest severe chastisement. He is the Master of all powers and is not restricted by man-made laws. He has power over everything, when His Wrath comes, the human mind cannot encompass its full scope, and none can then evade it.

In light of the attitude of certain people of the West or certain countries, Aḥmadīs should further turn to God. The Messiah[as] of God has also warned Europe, as well as America. The earthquakes, the storms, and the calamities that are occurring in the world are not specific to Asia. America has had a glimpse of it. Therefore, O Europe! You too are not safe. So have some fear of God and do not challenge the sense of Honour of God. I will also add here that Muslim countries, or those who are known as Muslim, should also reform their ways. Adopt ways and responses that present the high station and the good manners of the Holy Prophet[sa] to the world. This would then be the correct and befitting response of a believer.

The followers of the Promised Messiah[as] will establish the glory of Islam and the sanctity of the Holy Prophet[sa]

Now, what sort of an Islamic response is the one that is going on these days that you are killing your own countrymen, and destroying your own property? Islam does not allow abandoning absolute justice and fairness, even in enmity with other nations, and commands to employ wisdom. Let alone what has recently happened in Pakistan and is happening in other Muslim countries. In any case, these acts of damaging the businesses or embassies of other countries or acts of bringing harm to one's own people serve no purpose but to bring Islam in disrepute. Therefore, the Muslim masses should try and be wise rather than bring ruin upon themselves in this world, as well as, the Hereafter by following these erroneous religious scholars and leaders. Today, to determine the direction for Muslims, rather for the entire world, Allah has sent the true and ardent devotee of His beloved Holy Prophet[sa]. Accept him, follow him and join in the Community of the Messiah[as] to reform the world and to raise the banner of the Holy Prophet[sa] in the world. Now, no other way, no other guide can lead us to act upon and to implement the *Sunna* of the Holy Prophet[sa]. The restoration of the glory of Islam and the establishment of the sanctity of the Holy Prophet[sa] will now be done by and through the Community of the Promised Messiah and Mahdi[as] alone, *Inshā' Allāh*.

True meanings of the word *"Nuzūl-e-Masīḥ"*, some of the achievements of the Promised Messiah[as], and arguments in support of his truth

Hence, everyone should reflect, including those who are known as Muslims. We too should explain to them, and should not get embroiled in debates with the so-called religious scholars that the Messiah who had to come has not yet come or that he is to descend at such and such location. The fact is that the way in which this concept is presented is the result of not understanding a Hadith.

The Promised Messiah[as] has explained this tradition as follows, he says:

> If it is said that the Aḥadīth relate in clear and evident words that the Messiah, son of Mary, shall descend from the heavens and that his descent shall take place near the eastern minaret in Damascus and he will have his hands on the shoulders of two angels; then how could this specific and clear statement be denied?

That is to say, that this is what people say and as it is a clear and obvious statement, people ask, how could it be denied?

In response the Promised Messiah[as] stated:

> The answer to this is that descending from the heavens does not indicate that in reality a being would bodily come down, rather in the authentic Aḥadīth, even the word 'heavens' is not mentioned. Moreover the word *'nuzūl'* is commonly and widely used. When a person starts from one place to stop at another place, it is also said that he has descended here. Just as it is said that a troop has descended at such and such place or a convoy has descended. Is it understood from this that the troop or the convoy has come down from the heavens? Furthermore, Allah the Exalted has clearly declared in the Holy Qur'an that the Holy Prophet[sa] has also come down from the heavens. In fact at one point it is said that, 'We have caused iron to come

down from the heavens.' So it is quite clear that this descending from the heavens is not of the sort and nature, the sort that people imagine it to be.

(Izāla-e-Auhām, Rūḥānī Khazā'in, Vol. 3, pp. 132, 133)

The Promised Messiah[as] has said:

The Aḥadīth are replete with the explanation of this. People lack knowledge themselves, and the religious scholars mislead them.

He went on to further state:

For this the Jews also made the error and did not accept Ḥaḍrat 'Īsā[as].

In any case these are detailed and thorough matters which cannot be mentioned in the sermon. Aḥmadīs should try and explain these issues within their circles in accordance to the changing times so that as many auspicious souls as possible can be saved. All the decent people who can be saved, may be saved. Aḥmadīs should openly tell people of all religions within their circles that the one who was to come according to the teachings of all religions, has come.

The Promised Messiah[as] states:

I now present that Hadith to the audience that Abū Dā'ūd wrote in his Ṣaḥīḥ and draw their attention to its evidence. So, let it be clear that the Hadith that is recorded in Abū

Dā'ūd's Ṣaḥīḥ is that a person named Ḥārith shall come from *Ḥarrāth mā warā-'unnahar* i.e., from Samarkand who shall strengthen the people of the Prophet[sa], and whose help and victory will be binding for each believer. It has been Divinely revealed to me that this prophecy and the prophecy about the advent of the Messiah who will be the Imam of Muslims and will be from among them; in fact these two prophecies are common in their subject matter and this humble person alone is the substantiation of them both. In reality the key signs of the prophecy relating to the name of the Messiah are only two; one that when the Messiah will come he will reform the internal state of the Muslims, which will be extremely deteriorated at the time, with his right teachings.

This has been mentioned in earlier sermons. They (Muslim) accept that the condition of the Muslims is deteriorated and a reformer is needed.

Meaning of the term, "Masīḥ-e-Mau'ūd[as] (the Promised Messiah) will distribute treasures"

The Promised Messiah[as] said:

> Through his perfect teachings he will completely remove their spiritual destitution and inner penury and shall present them with treasures of erudition, truths and knowledge.

That is to say, these are the treasures and he shall elucidate spiritual knowledge to them.

He then said:

> So much so that people will get tired of receiving this wealth and no seeker of truth from among them will remain spiritually poor and indigent. All those who hunger and thirst for truth will be provided in abundance with the wholesome food of truth and the sweet drink of wisdom.

That is to say the pure diet of Truth will be given to them, the real teachings of Islam will be given to them only through the Promised Messiah[as] and the nectar of spiritual knowledge will be given to them. If these people were drinkers of the beverage of spiritual knowledge, they would not have reacted in the destructive, let alone unproductive way that has been demonstrated by them. Rather, they would have displayed a productive response and would have turned to God.

The Promised Messiah[as] states:

> ... and their pouches will be filled with the pearls of true knowledge.

The real knowledge of Islam is a precious treasure, it is like pearls, he will fill their pouches with it.

> They will be given a phial filled with the perfume of the true meaning of the Holy Qur'an.

They will receive the perfume of the Holy Qur'an.

Explanation of the terms, "Breaking of the Cross" and "Killing of the Swine"

The Promised Messiah[as] says:

> The second key sign is that when that Promised Messiah will come he shall break the Cross, kill the swine and kill the one-eyed *Dajjāl* . Every disbeliever who is touched by his breath will die instantly. The real interpretation of this special aspect is that the Messiah on arriving in this world will crush under his feet all the glory of the religion of the Cross, and that he shall destroy with the weapon of decisive arguments those who are afflicted with shamelessness and immodesty like swine, and who devour filth like pigs, and that he will wipe out with the sword of clear proofs the opposition of those who possess only worldly insight and are bereft of the eye of faith in place of which they have only an unsightly taint.

So these are the arguments with which the vanquishing is to be done so that the existence of their false claims can be finished off.

The Promised Messiah[as] further says:

> Not only such one-eyed people, but also every disbeliever who contemptuously looks down at Islam, will suffer spiritual extinction through the glorious breath of Messianic reasoning.

The Promised Messiah[as] will come and defeat them

with his reasoning.

> In short, all these statements are metaphorical, which have been unfolded very well to this humble person. Some may or may not understand it now but after waiting for sometime, and despairing altogether of the hopes of their baseless expectations that they now entertain, all of them will be inclined to this direction.
>
> (Izāla-e-Auhām, Rūḥānī Khazā'in, vol 3, pp. 141-143 footnotes)

In short, the Promised Messiah[as] has challenged the Christians in this age. It was him alone who stopped Christianity in its tracks as it was spreading fast. At that time, in India, hundreds of thousands of Muslims were turning to Christianity. It was only the Promised Messiah[as] who not only stopped their onslaught, rather also restored the honour of Islam. In addition, the Aḥmadiyya Muslim Community has stopped the onslaught of Christianity in Africa; demonstrated the beautiful picture of Islam to them and converted thousands of Christians to Islam. These were the achievements of the Messiah that the Promised Messiah[as] displayed and, with the Grace of God, it is with his teaching and reasoning that today the Aḥmadiyya Muslim Community is moving forward, winning the hearts, and *Inshā' Allāh* will keep on doing so. Just as the Promised Messiah[as] has said:

> One day these people will be disillusioned, and then will return.

So this is the explanation of how the deceit of these

people has to be ended. This is the meaning of killing the swine and breaking the Cross and the connotation of contesting the *Dajjāl* that the Promised Messiah[as] has explained.

As I have said earlier, it is the Aḥmadiyya Muslim Community alone that is contending with Christianity. Recently, there was a television programme on one of the TV channels (probably it was Geo or ARY channel, or some other similar Asian channel) in which one Allāmah Dr. Asrār said that because the Muslim religious people were illiterate and their religious knowledge was non-existent, both of the Holy Qur'an and the Bible, whereas Mirzā Ghulām Aḥmad Qādiānī was a scholarly man, and had knowledge of the Bible as well as of other religions, that is why he contended with the Christians and silenced them. His words (Dr. Asrār's) were to this effect. Anyway, he accepted that it was the Promised Messiah[as], who just as he himself has said, dismissed them with decisive arguments, strong arguments. They accept that it was Ḥaḍrat Mirzā Ghulām Aḥmad Qādiānī alone who halted the onslaughts of Christianity at the time and saved the Muslims from converting to Christianity. He (Dr. Asrār) then went on to give some senseless explanations, different explanations, he spoke a little against the Promised Messiah[as] that he could not be the Messiah. In any case, it is acknowledged today that if anyone stood up to Christianity and dismissed their teachings with arguments, it was just one champion, whose name is Mirzā Ghulām Aḥmad Qādiānī[as].

Therefore, whether these people today accept or not,

but just as the Promised Messiah[as] said one day they will have to accept that these are the Messianic arguments that thePromised Messiah[as] had presented and which demolished the *Dajjāl*, and he indeed is the Promised Messiah[as].

The Promised Messiah's advent had to be from *Ummat-e-Muslimah*

The Promised Messiah[as] has said that:

> The Muslims are still waiting for the Messiah due to inferring the wrong and apparent meaning of the Hadith that the Messiah, son of Mary, will descend from the heavens with his hands on the shoulders of angels.

Further elucidating that their inference is incorrect, the Promised Messiah[as] explains with reference to Hadith alone.

The Promised Messiah[as] states:

> One of the arguments which indicate that the Messiah to come, about whom this *ummah* has been promised, will be a person from this *ummah,* is the Hadith from Bukhārī and Muslim which states اِمَامُكُمْ مِّنْكُمْ and اَمَّكُمْ مِّنْكُمْ which means that he will be your Imam and will be from among you. Since this Hadith is regarding 'Īsā, who is to come and in this Hadith the words of *'Ḥakam'* - the arbitrator and *''Adal'* - the just, are present as attributes in his praise, which are used before this phrase. Therefore, the

word *'Imam'* is meant for him. There is no doubt that here in the word *'minkum'* the Companions[ra] are addressed and they alone were the intended addressee; obviously as none of them claimed to be the Promised Messiah. Therefore, *'minkum'* connotes a person who is a substitute for the Companions[ra] in the knowledge of Allah the Exalted.

That is, in Allah's sight, he has the status of the Companions[ra].

And it is him who has been stated as the substitute for the Companions[ra] in the under-mentioned verse, that is

وَ اٰخَرِيْنَ مِنْهُمْ لَمَّا يَلْحَقُوْا بِهِمْ ط [1]

62/4

This verse demonstrates that he is trained by the spirituality of the Holy Prophet[sa], and he is included in the Companions[ra] by virtue of this connotation. In elucidation of this verse is the Hadith:

لَوْ كَانَ الْاِيْمَانُ مُعَلَّقًا بِالثُّرَيَّا لَنَالَهٗ رَجُلٌ مِّنْ فَارِس [2]

And because tat quality has been attributed to this Persian person which is exclusive to the Promised Messiah and

1. And *among* others from among them who have not yet joined them. (Sūrah Al-Jumu'ah, 62:4)
2. If faith ascends to the Pleiades a man from Persia will bring it back. (Ṣaḥīḥ Bukhārī, Kitābut-Tafsīr Sūrah Al-Jumu'ah and Ṣaḥīḥ Muslim)

Mahdi, that is, to once again fill the earth with absolute justice, that having become devoid of faith and Unity of God has been filled with oppression; therefore, this person is the Mahdi and the Promised Messiah, and it is I.

(Tohfa-e-Golarhviyyah, Rūḥānī Khazā'in, Vol. 17, pp. 114-115)

Masīḥ and Mahdi are two names of the same person; abolition of religious wars by Masih Mau'ūd[as]

The Promised Messiah[as] further explains:

The Hadith

لَا مَهْدِیَّ اِلَّا عِیْسٰی [3]

from the book of *Ibn-e-Mājah*, which is well known by this very name, and is also comprised in the book *Mustadrak of Ḥākim*, where it is narrated by Anas bin Mālik. This tradition has been narrated by Muḥammad bin Khālid Al-Janadī on the authority of Abbān bin Ṣāleḥ, who related it on the authority of Ḥasan Baṣrī, who related it on the authority of Anas bin Mālik, who heard the Messenger[sa] of Allah say this. This Hadith means that there will be no Mahdi except the person who will appear in the spirit of

3. There is no Mahdī other than Jesus[as].

'Īsā. This means that the same person will be the Promised Messiah and Mahdi who will come in the spirit of Ḥaḍrat 'Īsā, peace be on him, and whose teachings will be like those of Ḥaḍrat 'Īsā[as]. This means that he will not physically resist evil nor fight; he will spread the truth through his holy example and heavenly signs. This Hadith is supported by another Hadith comprised in the collection of Ṣaḥīḥ Bukhārī by Imam Bukhārī, which says:

يَضَعُ الْحَرْبَ [4]

This means that the Mahdi, whose other name will be the Promised Messiah, will definitely suspend religious wars. He will instruct not to fight in the name of religion, rather to propagate religion through the light of truth, moral miracles and the signs of the nearness to God. I, therefore, affirm that he who fights in this age for the sake of religion, or lends support to any such fighter, openly or secretly, counsels fighting or entertain any such designs, is guilty of disobedience to God and the Messenger, and transgresses the limits, obligations and admonitions which are prescribed by them.

(Ḥaqīqat-ul-Mahdī, Rūḥānī Khazā'in, Vol. 14, pp. 431- 432)

You may observe that the current state of affairs of the Muslims is corroborating this. If these wars were according to the command of Allah the Exalted then Allah declares:

4. He will do away with wars.

وَكَانَ حَقًّا عَلَيْنَا نَصْرُ الْمُؤْمِنِيْنَ 0[5]

Therefore, when Allah's support is not there, things should be thought through. If they so wish to fight wars, at least they should not fight in the name of Islam.

The fact that the Muslims are being defeated by other nations in this era is also a practical testimony from God that the Messiah who was to come has come and the commandment for wars in the name of religion has been suspended under يَضَعُ الْحَرْبَ[6] Indeed, if you wish to engage in Jihad do so with arguments and reasoning. The consequences of the wars being fought by the Muslims in the name of Islam are – in accordance with the practical testimony of Allah – evident to all who have insight. Allah the Exalted has promised that He helps the believers if they are true believers. There can be two options; either these Muslims are not true believers or this is the wrong time for wars and that era has finished. Be mindful, these people comprise both of these aspects; for, by not listening to the Holy Prophet[sa] they cannot remain *momin* and owing to their non-acceptance, once the claim of the Promised Messiah[sa] is made, they are not rightfully due for Allah's help. So, the one who claimed to be the Messiah and the Mahdi in this era is truthful.

---

5. And it was certainly due from Us to help the believers. (Sūrah Al-Rūm, 30: 48).
6. He will do away with wars.

The sworn testimony of the Promised Messiah[as] that he has been appointed by God Almighty

Furthermore the Promised Messiah[as] made a huge claim of his truthfulness, a claim that a liar simply could not make.

He states:

> I swear by God Who has my life in His hand that He has sent me and He indeed has named me a Prophet and He indeed has called me with the name of Promised Messiah and He indeed has manifested a large number of great signs in my support which are numbered in three hundred thousand; some of which have been written in this book as an example. If His miraculous acts and manifest signs, which have reached in their thousands, did not bear witness to my truthfulness then I would have never revealed His dialogue to anyone and would not have been able to say with certainty that these are His words. However, He has exhibited such acts in support of His words that they have served as a clear and sparkling mirror to reveal His Countenance.
>
> (Tatimmah Ḥaqīqatul-Waḥī, Rūḥānī Khazā'in, Vol. 22, p. 503)

If the claim of one who makes a claim in the name of Allah the Exalted is not true, how does Allah treat him?

Observe that Allah has declared about a false prophet:

وَلَوْ تَقَوَّلَ عَلَيْنَا بَعْضَ الْاَقَاوِيْلِ 0 لَاَخَذْنَا مِنْهُ بِالْيَمِيْنِ 0

And if he had falsely *attributed* even a trivial statement to Us, We would surely have seized him by the right hand. (Sūrah Al-Ḥāqqah, 69:45 - 46)

And then God Almighty says:

ثُمَّ لَقَطَعْنَا مِنْهُ الْوَتِيْنَ ۝

And then surely We would have severed his jugular vein. (Sūrah Al-Ḥāqqah, 69: 47)

Now tell us, when the Promised Messiah[as] made the claim of prophethood and said that he had all the support of Allah, did Allah cut his jugular vein? Or has He in accordance to His promise:

وَكَانَ حَقًّا عَلَيْنَا نَصْرُ الْمُؤْمِنِيْنَ ۝ [7]

helped him and continues to help the Community? A voice that arose from a small hamlet is today spread to the corners of the world with full glory. Today the Aḥmadiyya Muslim Community is established in 181 countries.

Today, the followers of the Promised Messiah[as] are found in Europe, in America and in the far flung jungles and scorching deserts of Africa and as well as in the islands. Is all this Divine support not sufficient to believe in his

---

7. And it was certainly due from Us to help the believers. (Sūrah Al-Rūm, 30:48)

truthfulness? If this person was false, then why did Allah not seize him in accordance to His laws? Why has He not destroyed him for attributing Divine revelations to himself? It is time to reflect. Reflect and be wise. I ask the Muslims why are they ruining their life in this world and the Hereafter? The fate of a false person is such that recently someone claimed to be the Mahdi in Pakistan, after exchanging some gunfire they arrested him and he is now imprisoned. The ending to this came quickly to the fore; there were many others before this.

Heavenly signs in support of the Promised Messiah[as]

There is also a heavenly sign of his truthfulness which I have mentioned before; that is the solar and lunar eclipse. This is a sign that could have no possible human interference. 1400 years ago the Holy Prophet[sa] prophesied in a specific manner, and informed us that in this specific manner - in this day and age, now that science has greatly advanced, the predictions about the near future, let alone the distant future cannot be made - that it will be the month of Ramadan, that a solar eclipse will occur on such and such date, and a lunar eclipse will occur on such and such date.

The Hadith states:

اِنَّ لِمَهْدِيِّنَا اٰيَتَيْنِ لَمْ تَكُوْنَا مُنْذُ خَلْقِ السَّمٰوٰتِ وَالْاَرْضِ

تَنْكَسِفُ الْقَمَرُ لِاَوَّلِ لَيْلَةٍ مِّنْ رَمَضَانَ وَ تَنْكَسِفُ الشَّمْسُ فِى النِّصْفِ مِنْهُ

(Sunan Dār Quṭnī, Kitābul 'Eīdain, Bābu Ṣifati Ṣalātil Khusūfī)

That is, there are only two signs of the truthfulness of Our Mahdi, and since the earth came into being these signs of truthfulness have never appeared before. In Ramadan the lunar eclipse will occur on the first night of the nights of lunar eclipse and the solar eclipse will occur on the middle day of the days of solar eclipse.

It was in 1894 that this eclipse occurred. Between the dates of 13th, 14th, and 15th Ramadan the lunar eclipse occurred on the 13th and from the dates of 27th, 28th, and 29th the solar eclipse occurred on 28th Ramadan. This is very clear proof of his truthfulness.

The Promised Messiah[as] has said that at the time there was no other claimant apart from him. Some *maulavīs* argue about [the word] *"Qamar"* etc. According to some *"Qamar"* is the moon of the night following the second night and according to others it is the moon of the night following the third night. Let them show if there was a claim other than that of the Promised Messiah[as] before this corroborating sign appeared. If there is a claim, it is that of just one person; Ḥaḍrat Mirzā Ghulām Aḥmad Qādiānī. The Promised

Messiah[as] has clearly stated that numerous signs have been fulfilled, if it is not him, then, let's see who else has come because it certainly is the need of the hour. However, these people cannot comply, as the Promised Messiah[as] alone, is the true claimant because he is supported by worldly and heavenly substantiations. The Divinely explained standard of prophethood supports him. Many people have accepted in the past that he had a pure and chaste character. His past was pure, and his youth was pure. He was scholarly and no one else served Islam as he did. The outsiders have accepted this. Despite having witnessed all this, if they are still confused then God help them, because it is with God's Grace alone that the capacity to believe in someone is granted.

The Promised Messiah[as] writes:

> Let them say, if this humble person is not being truthful, who else came, who claimed in a way as did this humble person, to be the *Mujaddid* at the onset of the 14th century. Did anyone rise, armed with Divinely revealed prayers, against all the opponents as this humble person did?
>
> تَفَكَّرُوْا وَتَنَدَّمُوْا وَاتَّقُوْا اللّٰهَ وَلَا تَغْلُوْا
>
> That is, ponder about it, have some shame; fear Allah. Why do you exceed limits in brazenness?
>
> If this humble person is at fault to claim as the Promised Messiah then you people should make some endeavours so that the one who, in your opinion is the Promised Messiah, descends from the heavens one of these days. I am around

> at the moment, however the one you await is not around. My claim can be invalidated only in the event that he descends from the heavens so that I am branded a criminal.

This is the challenge he gave at the time to everyone.

> If you people are on the truth then you should pray collectively that the Messiah, son of Mary, is soon observed descending from the heavens. If you are truthful, then this prayer will be accepted because the prayer of the truthful is accepted against the prayer of liars.

This means that compared to a liar's prayers, those of a truthful one are accepted.

> However, you may be absolutely assured that this prayer will certainly not be accepted because you are in the wrong. The Messiah has come but you have not recognised him. Now this imaginary hope of yours will never be fulfilled. This age will pass and none among them will see the Messiah descend.

(Izāla-e-Auhām Part 1, Rūḥānī Khazā'in, Vol. 3, p. 179)

The Promised Messiah[as] furher says:

> This is the reason why I say that these people are the enemies of religion and truth. If a party of these people were to reform their hearts and come to me even now, I am still prepared to remove their absurd and nonsensical doubts. I would demonstrate to them how God has facilitated prophecies like a vast army, as proof of my claim, which manifest the truth like daybreak.

Allah, the Almighty has promised to establish love of the Promised Messiah[as] in the hearts of the people and make his sect dominant over all other sects

Just as the Promised Messiah[as] had said if anyone wishes to come, today, after a hundred years, the condition to come with reformed heart stands. Those who come do find the truth.

He said:

> If these foolish *maulavīs* deliberately close their eyes then so be it. Truth will not lose out due to them. However, that time is near, rather it is imminent that many inordinate conceits, Pharaoh like-minded, will be saved from destruction by reflecting on these prophecies. Allah commands that I shall execute attack upon attack until such a time that I shall embed your truth in hearts.
>
> Therefore, O *maulavīs*, if you have the power to fight with God, then fight. Before my time, the Jews mistreated the poor man, son of Mary most extraordinarily and in their conjecture they put him on the Cross. However, God saved him from death on the Cross. There was a time when he was only thought of as cunning and a liar, and now a time has come that his greatness has been inculcated in hearts to an extent that 40 million people believe him to be god. Although, these people have been blasphemous in that they have made a humble man god, but this is the answer to the Jews. The person whom they wanted to crush underneath

their feet as a liar, the very same Jesus, son of Mary, has reached the greatness that 40 million people prostrate before him and Kings bow down to him. I have therefore prayed that like Jesus, son of Mary, I do not become a means of promoting *shirk*. I am fully sure that God will do so. However, Allah the Exalted has repeatedly informed me that He will give me much greatness and shall inculcate my love in hearts and will spread my mission over the entire earth and shall give my sect triumph over all other sects. People of my sect will acquire excellence in knowledge and spiritual cognisance to a degree that they will silence everyone with the light of their truthfulness and with their reasoning and signs.

With the Grace of Allah this truth is being exhibited in each country of the world and is continuing to do so.

Each body of people will drink from this fountain and this mission shall grow mightily and shall expand until such a time that it will envelop the earth. Many obstacles will come about and turmoils will come to pass but God shall remove them all, and shall fulfil His promise. God has addressed me and pronounced, 'I shall grant you blessing upon blessing so much so that Kings shall seek blessings from your garments.'

The Promised Messiah[as] further says:

Hearken! O' those who care to hear, remember these words and safeguard these prophecies in your trunks for these are the words of God which will be fulfilled one day. I see no virtue in my self and I have not done the task that I should have done. I consider myself an unworthy peasant. It is merely Allah's Grace that favoured my circumstances. A

> thousand-fold gratitude to the Powerful and Noble God that He accepted this handful of dust despite all the ineptness.
>
> (Tajalliyyāt-e Ilāhiyyah, Rūḥānī Khazā'in, Vol. 20, pp. 408-410)

Whether it is the claim or the prophecy of the Promised Messiah[as], we see it being fulfilled daily. However, this is also a juncture at which each nation and religion should reflect and ponder. The Community of the Promised Messiah[as] is continually progressing in accordance to the Divine promises, and as I said, we observe this progress daily. So the Muslims too should reflect (that is the Muslims, aside from the Aḥmadīs) that the Messiah and Mahdi who was to come has come. There are numerous proofs in the Holy Qur'an and Aḥādīth for his truthfulness. These can be found in the Holy Qur'an as well as in Hadith, and I have mentioned one or two of them. The condition of the world too is calling out for him. Who do you await for now? O people! Ponder a little. The Messiah who was to have a second-coming for the Christians has also come. The advent of one who was to gather people of all religions on one hand has taken place. Now it is this Messiah and Mahdi alone who will teach you how to show respect for each other. If anyone is to teach respect for the Prophets of all religions, it is this Promised Messiah[as]. If love and peace is to be spread in the world it will be through this Promised Messiah[as]. If humanity is to be delivered from pain and suffering it will be through this Promised Messiah and Mahdi[as]. If the ways leading to Allah are to be shown and the modes to turn to God are to be told, these will happen through this Promised Messiah[as] alone. If the world seeks all this, then they must stick to the teachings of the one whose coming was foretold by all the Prophets and who is the true and ardent devotee of the Holy Prophet[sa]. Otherwise we can see the shadows of Allah's severe chastisement hovering, that the Promised Messiah[as], after being told by God, informed us about. I will say to you, who are Aḥmadīs, that each Aḥmadī should pay attention towards reforming themselves and as you reform yourselves make the world aware of Allah's severe chastisement as well. May Allah have mercy on these worldly people and enable them to see the Truth.

(3)

Friday Sermon Delivered on 24th February, 2006 at Baitul Futūh Mosque, Morden, London, UK

****

(3)

Friday Sermon Delivered on 24th February, 2006

- Description of the cruel attitude and hurting of the sentiments of the Muslims by certain Western countries and newspapers under the disguise of freedom of press and freedom of conscience, and exposure of their double standards.

- The daring degrading attacks by the Western world upon the Muslims are the result of the plight of the internal condition of the Muslims, and the Muslim world is facing extremely dangerous situation as a result of their own mistakes.

- Love of the Holy Prophet[sa] demands from us that we earnestly pray for *Ummat-e-Muslimah* in our prayers. It is duty of each Aḥmadī who has accepted the Imam of the age that due to extreme love of the Holy Prophet[sa], they invoke blessing upon the Holy Prophet[sa], in abundance.

- You should spread so much *Durūd*, invoked from the bottom of your heart, in the atmosphere that each particle in the atmosphere shines out from far away, and all our prayers through intercession of this *Durūd* reach to and is accepted by God Almighty.

- Importance of invoking *Durūd* upon the Holy Prophet[sa] according to the Holy Qur'an, the traditions of the Holy Prophet[sa] and sayings of the Promised Messiah[as], and special appeal to invoke *Durūd* upon the Holy Prophet[sa], in abundance, and to pray for the *Ummat-e-Muslimah.*

****

اَشْهَدُ اَنْ لاَّ اِلٰهَ اِلاَّ اللّٰهُ وَحْدَهٗ لاَ شَرِيْكَ لَهٗ وَ اَشْهَدُ اَنَّ مُحَمَّدًا عَبْدُهٗ وَرَسُوْلُهٗ .

اَمَّا بَعْدُ فَاَعُوْذُ بِاللّٰهِ مِنَ الشَّيْطٰنِ الرَّجِيْمِ

بِسْمِ اللّٰهِ الرَّحْمٰنِ الرَّحِيْمِ ٥

اَلْحَمْدُ لِلّٰهِ رَبِّ الْعٰلَمِيْنَ ٥ الرَّحْمٰنِ الرَّحِيْمِ ٥ مٰلِكِ يَوْمِ الدِّيْنِ ٥ اِيَّاكَ نَعْبُدُ وَاِيَّاكَ نَسْتَعِيْنُ ٥ اِهْدِنَا الصِّرَاطَ الْمُسْتَقِيْمَ ٥ صِرَاطَ الَّذِيْنَ اَنْعَمْتَ عَلَيْهِمْ ٥ غَيْرِ الْمَغْضُوْبِ عَلَيْهِمْ وَلاَ الضَّآلِّيْنَ ٥

اِنَّ اللّٰهَ وَمَلٰٓئِكَتَهٗ يُصَلُّوْنَ عَلَى النَّبِيِّ ط يٰٓاَيُّهَا الَّذِيْنَ اٰمَنُوْا صَلُّوْا عَلَيْهِ وَسَلِّمُوْا تَسْلِيْمًا ٥

I bear witness that there is none worthy of worship except Allah and He is One and has no partner. And I bear witness that Muḥammad is His Servant and Messenger.

After this, I seek refuge with Allah from Satan, the rejected

In the Name of Allah, the Gracious, the Merciful

All praise belongs to Allah, Lord of all the worlds. The Gracious, the Merciful. Master of the Day of Judgment. Thee alone do we worship and Thee alone do we implore for help. Guide us in the right path -- The path of those on whom Thou has bestowed *Thy* blessings, those who have not incurred displeasure, and those who have not gone astray. (Sūrah Al-Fātiḥah, 1:1-7)

Allah and His angels send blessings on the Prophet. O ye who believe! you *also* should invoke blessings on *him* and salute him with the salutation of peace. (Sūrah Al-Aḥzāb, 33:57)

I shall carry on with the previous subject concerning the events, which have been happening for the past few weeks. Today, again, I will briefly speak about the wicked attitude of some newspapers of the West that they have initiated in the name of freedom of the press and freedom of conscience. This is hurtful to the sentiments of Muslims. I also want to talk about the protests which are going on in Muslim countries at the individual, communal as well as governmental level against some newspapers. In fact the OIC (Organisation of Islamic Countries) has said that the Western countries will be pressured to apologise as well as to legislate against offending Prophets of God in the name of freedom of the press and freedom of conscience. If they do not abstain, then world peace could not be guaranteed. It is a very good response from these countries and the OIC. May Allah strengthen the Muslim countries and enable them to be capable of getting such decisions made for world peace with sincerity of heart.

Double-standards of the Western countries and newspapers

Recently, an Iranian newspaper announced that, as a reprisal, it would arrange a contest to have cartoons made with reference to the Holocaust. Although this is not an Islamic response, and is not an Islamic way, however, the Western newspapers who seemingly champion freedom and publish all sorts of nonsense in the name freedom of speech, should not have been as upset as they have been. Either they should not have been upset or they should have said in response that the mistake has created turmoil in the world. We should now put an end to this kind of viewpoint about any religion or its founder or Prophet, or any nation and create an environment of love. However, rather than giving such a response, the editor of the Danish newspaper, which published the caricatures that instigated the disorder around the world, has responded to the Iranian announcement regarding the contest for the Holocaust caricatures. He said that this contest would have been about the possibility whether the Holocaust had occurred or not. It would not have been about offending or defaming any Prophet. Anyway, the newspaper editor writes that we shall certainly not participate in the contest. While reassuring his readers, he says that our readers should rest assured that our moral standards are maintained. We are not one to publish a cartoon about Jesus[as] or the Holocaust. Therefore there is no question about us participating under any circumstances in the bad-taste contest of the Iranian newspaper and media. So, these are their standards; one for themselves and another to trifle with the sentiments of Muslims. Such are their deeds; they may carry on!

The extremely pitiful plight of Muslims

Observe the state of their standards. Recently, when a British author went to Austria, he was imprisoned there for three years following a court case for something he had written seventeen years ago. So these are their ways. They have no tolerance in their own matters. However, we too should analyse our own condition. Could the audacity that the West is developing be due to our own condition? It is obvious from what we see that the Western world is aware that the Muslims are under their subjugation. After all is said and done, Muslims come to them in the end. They seek help from these people to fight amongst themselves. They know that the current boycott on the products of some European countries as a mark of protest is only going to last a short while. The products that have been removed from the shops and are not on sale currently will be back on sale in these countries. After all the Muslims living in these [European] countries are consuming these products. There are about 200,000 Muslims in Demark (against which the biggest protest has been made), and a huge majority of them are Pakistani Muslims. After all, they are using these things. In any case these are transitory reactions that shall dwindle away.

Now look at our own condition; the recent incident in Iraq in which the dome of an *Imam Bārgāh* (shrine) was blown away in a bomb blast. As a result of this, Sunnī mosques are now being attacked and destroyed. No one has tried to stop and think to investigate whether this was a mischievous plot by the enemy to rile them up against each other. All the bombs and other weapons which they are receiving are being provided by these countries. However, they cannot think in this way; for one, they lose their senses. In rage and sectarian prejudice, they can't think of what to do. Besides, those, who unfortunately are hypocrites, join the enemy and the enemy takes advantage of this and does not let them think things over.

In any case, this new situation that has developed in Iraq is taking the country towards civil war. It has all but started these days. The leaders there are facing great difficulty in controlling the situation. Muslims are fighting Muslims in Afghanistan as well. In Pakistan also, each sect tries to terrorize the other sect. They kill each other in the name of religion. Whereas Allah the Exalted states:

وَمَنْ يَّقْتُلْ مُؤْمِنًا مُّتَعَمِّدًا فَجَزَآءُهٗ جَهَنَّمُ خَالِدًا فِيْهَا
وَغَضِبَ اللّٰهُ عَلَيْهِ وَلَعَنَهٗ وَاَعَدَّ لَهٗ عَذَابًا عَظِيْمًا 0

And whoso kills a believer intentionally, his reward shall be Hell wherein he shall abide. And Allah will be wroth with him and will curse him and will prepare for him a great punishment. (Sūrah Al-Nisā', 4:94)

The real cause of Muslim's fragmentation and weakness is their disobedience of the Holy Prophet[sa] and refusal to accept the Promised Messiah[as]

Observe, they are killing each other on the instigation of their seditious, provocative leaders, the majority of whom are religious leaders. All these mischiefs have been started by them. There is violence and murder, and they are being told that if they kill they would earn a reward and will enter Paradise. Whereas, Allah is cursing them and sending them to Hell.

In Pakistan, Bangladesh and other countries where Aḥmadīs are being martyred, it is these [religious leaders] who give the incitement of entering Paradise and make them do hellish tasks. Anyway, I was saying that the enemies of Muslims take advantage of the misdemeanours of the Muslims and diminish the power of the Muslims, and the Muslims do not realise it. Anyway, it is quite clear that the reason they have lost their senses and are so blighted is because they have not obeyed the commandment of the Holy Prophet[sa], and they are neither obeying it nor paying any attention to this. They are denying the Promised Messiah[as]. Every Aḥmadī should pray to Allah the Exalted. Earlier, I have drawn attention to this, that may Allah give them wisdom that they may not become those who bring Islam in disrepute by becoming an instrument of the hypocrites and the enemies, and kill each other.

In any case, when the enemy of Islam tries to disgrace and dishonour these Muslims one way or the other, an Aḥmadī feels pain because these people are attributed to, or claim to be attributed to, our beloved, the Holy Prophet[sa]. No doubt it is due to their lack of knowledge that a vast majority of these misled Muslims are deceived by these leaders and religious scholars, and thus they commit inappropriate acts that have absolutely no connection with Islam. May Allah, in acceptance of our prayers, release these people from the claws of these so-called religious leaders. May they understand the beautiful teachings of Islam, and whether unwittingly or foolishly, and in the passion of the love of Islam do not become the source of notoriety for Islam, as they are. May Allah guide them to the right path, because due to their improprieties the enemy of Islam gets a chance to abuse Islam as well as gets a chance to make offensive attacks on the person of the Holy Prophet[sa].

Each Aḥmadī should pay great attention to prayers these days because due to its own mistakes the world of Islam is suffering from most frightening circumstances. If we have true love and devotion for the Holy Prophet[sa], then we should pray abundantly for the *ummah.* We need to pay attention to this, which we are already in the process of.

The real way of supplicating and receiving blessings

However, today I wish to draw attention to the way in

which we should pray. These ways and modes of praying are also taught to us by the Holy Prophet[sa], which not only reform us, but also make us experience the acceptance of prayers.

According to a Hadith, which is related by Ḥaḍrat 'Umar bin Khaṭṭāb[ra] relates, the Holy Prophet[sa] said that prayer stops in between the earth and the heavens, and unless salutations and blessings are invoked *(Durūd)* on the Holy Prophet[sa] no portion of the prayer reaches above (to be presented to Allah).

(Sunan Tirmadhī, Kitāb-uṣ-Ṣalāti, Bābu mā Jā'a fī Faḍliṣ-Ṣalāti 'alan-Nabiyyi)

This is a reality about which Allah the Exalted has also clearly explained to us in the Holy Qur'an, that is in the verse I just recited:

إِنَّ اللّٰهَ وَمَلٰٓئِكَتَهٗ يُصَلُّوْنَ عَلَى النَّبِيِّ ۗ يٰٓاَيُّهَا الَّذِيْنَ اٰمَنُوْا

صَلُّوْا عَلَيْهِ وَسَلِّمُوْا تَسْلِيْمًا 0

Allah and His angels send blessings on the Prophet. O ye who believe! you *also* should invoke blessings on him and salute *him* with the salutation of peace. (Sūrah Al-Aḥzāb, 33:57)

In the Holy Qur'an, numerous commandments are given to follow. Following them makes one dear to Allah, the recipient of His blessings, closer to Him, the recipient of protection from Hell and of entry into Paradise. The commandment here refers to a task, which is so tremendous and great that Allah the Exalted has engaged his angels to do the job, and He Himself also invokes blessings and salutations on His beloved Prophet[sa]. This is an act by following which one would be following the task that is an act of Allah. When Allah the Exalted grants us immense rewards for abiding by His commandments, imagine the reward for following something that He Himself engages in. Most certainly, the *Durūd* invoked with sincerity of the heart would be a source of the reformation of the *ummah*, a source of protecting the *ummah* from disgrace, a source of our own reformation, a means of acceptance of our prayers, and also a basis of our protection from the evil of the *Dajjāl*.

In the Aḥādīth, the benefits of *Durūd* are mentioned under various narrations.

In one Tradition, the Holy Prophet[sa] said:

> On the Day of Judgment the person who sends the most blessings on me will be the closest to me.
>
> (Sunan Tirmadhī, Kitāb-us-Ṣalāti, Bābu mā Jā'a fī Faḍliṣ-Ṣalāti 'alan-Nabiyyi)

He[sa] also said that:

> Allah will send blessings ten times on the one who once invokes *Durūd* with the sincerity of heart. Allah will elevate his status ten-fold (and shall register ten virtues for

him), and forgive his ten sins.

(Sunan An-Nasa'ī, Kitāb-us-Sahvi, Bābul-Faḍli fiṣ-Ṣalāti 'alan-Nabiyyi)

Thus, the proviso is sincerity of the heart. Many who pray or ask for prayers write that we are praying a lot, you are also praying and we also invoke blessings but a long period has gone by and our prayers are not accepted.

The Holy Prophet[sa] explained how to invoke *Durūd.* He said:

صَادِقًا مِّنْ نَّفْسِهٖ Send *Durūd,* with absolute sincerity.

While invoking blessings each person should scrutinize themselves, scrutinize their hearts as to how much of this world's contamination is in it and how much sincerity of the heart there is in sending the *Durūd.*

The Promised Messiah[as] states about this:

Durūd, which is a tremendous source of achieving steadfastness, invoke it abundantly. However, do not recite it customarily or habitually, rather, do it by keeping in view the splendour and favours of the Holy Prophet[sa]; for the elevation of his status and station and for his triumphs. The result of this will be that you will be given the sweet and delicious fruit of the acceptance of prayer.

(Review of Religions, Urdu, Vol. 3, No. 1, p. 115)

So, these are the ways to invoke *Durūd*.

He[as] further says:

> O people! Invoke blessings on this benefactor Prophet[sa] who is a manifestation of the Gracious and great Benefactor God, for the recompense of favour is favour. The heart that has no appreciation of his favours either has no faith or is in pursuit to destroy the faith. O Allah! Send blessings and salutation on the un-lettered Prophet and Messenger who has satiated the latter ones, just as he satiated the earlier ones, and coloured them in his hue and linked them with pure people.
>
> (Translation from Arabic: E'ijāz-ul-Masīḥ, Rūḥānī Khazā'in, vol. 18 pp. 5-6)

If you invoked blessings in the manner that it took on a collective hue, it would be the kind of *Durūd* that manifests its effectiveness. This Hadith and the words of the Promised Messiah[as] should clarify the matter to those who say that *Durūd* is not effective and they should never tire of invoking blessings and salutations, rather they should self-reflect.

The Holy Prophet[sa] has said:

> The one who does not invoke blessings on him is very niggardly, is a miser. Not only is he putting the sin of niggardliness on himself through his miserliness, he is also being deprived of Allah's blessings. Just as we have seen that Allah sends ten-fold blessings on the person who

invokes blessings once.

(Jalā'ul -Afhām, p 318, quoted in Sunan An-Nasā'ī)

This way of attaining God's refuge is such a bargain that the Companions[ra] of the Holy Prophet[sa] and some Companions[ra] of the Promised Messiah[as] would set aside all other prayers and would only engage in *Durūd.*

In one Tradition, the Holy Prophet[sa] said:

> It would be a matter of insolence and disloyalty if I was mentioned around a person and that person did not send blessings and salutations on me.

(Jalā'ul -Afhām, p. 327, Published in 1897, Amritsar)

Ḥaḍrat Abū Bakr[ra] said:

> Invoking blessings on the Holy Prophet[sa] is of more excellence than freeing someone from the gallows, and that his companionship is more venerable than giving one's life in Allah's cause or to engage in Jihad.

(Tafsīr Durr-e-Manthūr, quoted in Tārīkh-e-Khatīb and Targhīb-e- Isfahānī; quoted in 'Durūd Sharīf', p 160)

The so-called Jihad of today which includes fighting others as well as fighting and slaughtering each other, one should ask these religious scholars as to what sort of Islam it is through which they misguide and incite the uneducated and illiterate Muslims (who then go on to carry out erroneous activities in their religious fervour and honour for Islam). The teaching of Islam is that when one hears unbefitting words about the Holy Prophet[sa], one should relate his[sa] qualities, and send blessings on him[sa]. This is more venerable than their Jihad. It is much better to focus on prayers and invoking blessings than giving one's life.

In this era, which is the era of the Promised Messiah[as], it is all the more important that rather than violence, focus is put on prayers and invoking blessings as well as to try and reform oneself. Scrutinise your inner self as to how much do we love the Holy Prophet[sa]. Could it be a transitory ardour that is enveloping us in a fire on account of the selfish motives of certain groups?

It is therefore, needed that while we concentrate on reforming ourselves, if we can, we also must make the Muslims within our circle understand not to adopt wrong ways rather to adopt the way that is favoured by Allah and His Messenger[sa]. That way has been explained to us and it is that the Holy Prophet[sa] has said that if you want to attain my pleasure and go to Paradise then invoke blessings on me.

Ḥaḍrat 'Abdullāh bin Mas'ūd[ra] relates that the Holy Prophet[sa] said:

The person who does not send blessings and salutations on

me has no faith.

(Jalā'ul -Afhām, quoted by Muḥammad bin Ḥamadān Marūzī)

At another occasion he[sa] said:

> Remembering Allah in abundance and sending blessings on me is a source of removing hardship.
>
> (Jalā'ul-Afhām, Faṣlul Mauṭinis-Sādisi wal-'Ishrūna min Mawāṭiniṣ-Ṣalāti 'Alaihi Ṣallallāhu 'alaihi wasallam 'Indal-ma'mil-Faqri wal-Ḥājati au Khaufin)

Financial hardship, circumstantial hardship, all the hardships that are befalling Muslims today are due to the fact that the West has one set of principles for themselves and another set of principles for the Muslims. The best solution for this is to invoke utmost blessings and salutations on the Holy Prophet[sa] and benefit from the blessings that Allah the Exalted has associated with *Durūd.*

In a Tradition (a section of which was mentioned before) which is detailed elsewhere as well, Ḥaḍrat Anas[ra] relates that the Holy Prophet[sa] said:

> On the Day of Judgment at each dreadful phase of the Day, that person will be the closest to me who would have sent the most blessings on me in the world.
>
> (Tafsīr Durr-e-Manthūr, quoted by Sha'bul-Īmāni lil-Baihaqī and Tārīkh Ibn-e-'Asākir)

Who does not wish to have the nearness of the Holy Prophet[sa] on the Day of Judgment and go through each dangerous phase under his protection? Certainly everyone wants to be protected from Allah's Wrath, and this is the way to be saved and to retain the nearness to the Holy Prophet[sa] which he[sa] has told us about. Therefore a believer should always be focused towards invoking blessings and should take every opportunity to say *Durūd*.

In a Tradition related by Ḥaḍrat Anas[ra] the Holy Prophet[sa] said:

> The person who will send blessings and salutations on me a thousand times a day will sight his station in Paradise while in this world.

(Jilā'ul-Afhām, quoted by Ibnul-Ghāzī and Kitābuṣ-Ṣalāti 'Alan-Nabiyyi li-Abī Abdillāhil-Maqdasī)

The transformations brought about by the blessings of invoking *Durūd* will make one's life on the earth heavenly. Furthermore, it is these good deeds and pious acts, which will make the present life heavenly, as well as these will make one the recipient of Paradise in the Hereafter.

A Tradition narrated by Ḥaḍrat 'Abdullāh bin 'Amr bin al-'Āṣ[ra] relates that he heard the Holy Prophet[sa] say:

> When you hear the *muedhdhin* calling for prayer you should repeat his words, then send blessings on me. Allah sends ten-fold blessings on a person who invokes blessings

and salutations on me. He then said, 'Seek mediation for me as this is a status from among the ranks of Paradise which will be given to one person from among Allah's servants and I have hope that it will be I. Intercession will be *Ḥalāl* for whoever will seek mediation for me.'

(Ṣaḥīḥ Muslim, Kitāb-uṣ-Ṣalāti Bābustiḥbābil Qauli mithla Qaulil Mu'adhdhini liman sami'ahū Thumma yuṣallī 'Alan-Nabiyyi)

Each Aḥmadī should learn and read the prayer said after the *Adhān*. The significance and benefits of sending blessings and salutations have now been clarified, however, some people also ask which kind of *Durūd* should they say? There are different versions of *Durūd* invoked by different people. However, there is a Hadith in this regard.

Ḥaḍrat Ka'b 'Ujrah[ra] narrates that we submitted:

O Prophet of Allah! We know about sending salutations on you but how do we invoke *Durūd* on you?

He replied, say:

اَللّٰهُمَّ صَلِّ عَلٰى مُحَمَّدٍ وَّ عَلٰى اٰلِ مُحَمَّدٍ كَمَا صَلَّيْتَ عَلٰى
اِبْرَاهِيْمَ اِنَّكَ حَمِيْدٌ مَّجِيدٌ - وَ بَارِكْ عَلٰى مُحَمَّدٍ وَّ عَلٰى اٰلِ
مُحَمَّدٍ كَمَا بَارَكْتَ عَلٰى اِبْرَاهِيْمَ اِنَّكَ حَمِيْدٌ مَّجِيدٌ

O Allah, Bless Muḥammad and the people of Muḥammad as You did bless Abraham. You are indeed the Praiseworthy, the Glorious. And prosper Muḥammad and the people of Muḥammad as You did prosper Abraham. You are indeed the Praiseworthy, the Glorious.

(Sunan Tirmadhī, Kitābuṣ-Ṣalāti, Abwābul Witri, Bābu mā jā'a fī Ṣifatiṣ-Ṣalāti 'Alan- Nabiyyi Ṣallallāhu 'alaihi wasallam)

So this is *Durūd*. The *Durūd* we say in *Ṣalāt* is a little more detailed. The Promised Messiah[as] counsels someone in a letter regarding this matter and writes:

Keep engaged in *Tahajjud* Prayer and commonly repeated prayers. There are many blessings in *Tahajjud*. Idleness is worthless. An idle and laid back [person] carries no weight. God Almighty says:

وَالَّذِيْنَ جَاهَدُوْا فِيْنَا لَنَهْدِيَنَّهُمْ سُبُلَنَا ط [8]

The preferred *Durūd* is, which was uttered by the blessed tongue of the Holy Prophet[sa] and that is:

اَللّٰهُمَّ صَلِّ عَلٰى مُحَمَّدٍ وَّ عَلٰى اٰلِ مُحَمَّدٍ كَمَا صَلَّيْتَ عَلٰى
اِبْرَاهِيْمَ وَ عَلٰى اٰلِ اِبْرَاهِيْمَ اِنَّكَ حَمِيْدٌ مَّجِيْدٌ

8. And *as for* those who strive in Our path --- We will surely guide them in Our ways. (Sūrah Al-'Ankabūt, 29:70)

اَللّٰھُمَّ بَارِكْ عَلٰى مُحَمَّدٍ وَّ عَلٰى اٰلِ مُحَمَّدٍ كَمَا بَارَكْتَ

عَلٰى اِبْرَاھِيْمَ وَ عَلٰى اٰلِ اِبْرَاھِيْمَ اِنَّكَ حَمِيْدٌ مَّجِيْدٌ [9]

He said:

> The words said by a pious person certainly have a lot of blessings in them. It should, therefore, be understood how blessed would be the words uttered by one who is the chief of the righteous and the commander of the Prophets. In short, from all the versions of *Durūd* this one is the most blessed one.

There are different versions of *Durūd* and this is the most blessed one.

> This is the chant of this humble person and it is not important to restrict it to any amount. [It] should be recited with sincerity, love and humility and should be recited until such time that one develops a state of tender-heartedness, is entranced and inspired, feels deep conviction, and discernment in the breast.

(Maktūbāt-e-Aḥmadiyya, Vol. 1, pp. 17-18)

---

9. O Allah, Bless Muḥammad and the people of Muḥammad as You did bless Abraham and the people of Abraham. You are indeed the Praiseworthy, the Glorious.

O Allah, Prosper Muḥammad and the people of Muḥammad as You did prosper Abraham and the people of Abraham. You are indeed the Praiseworthy, the Glorious.

This is the *Durūd* that we say in the *Ṣalāt,* and as I said this should be mostly recited. The Promised Messiah[as] has said not to focus on how many times it is said.

It is mentioned in a Hadith that reciting it a thousand times signifies the maximum one recites. Yet, the Promised Messiah[as] also suggested a specific number to some people; to say it seven hundred times daily to some or eleven hundred times to others. This advice is specific to individuals according to their situation and standard, which keeps on changing. In any case we should invoke *Durūd* and this is the reason why in the prayers for the [Khilāfat] Jubilee I had asked you to recite daily the revealed prayer of the Promised Messiah[as]:

سُبْحَانَ اللّٰهِ وَبِحَمْدِهٖ ، سُبْحَانَ اللّٰهِ الْعَظِيْمِ ۔ اَللّٰهُمَّ صَلِّ

عَلٰى مُحَمَّدٍ وَّ اٰلِ مُحَمَّدٍ ۔[10]

Besides this, I had said that *Durūd* should be recited in its entirety. The reason for this was that we should definitely include the authentic *Durūd* that was taught by the Holy Prophet[sa] in our prayers. However, the fact remains, as the Promised Messiah[as] said, that it should be recited with such profundity that it brings on a unique state of mind and when

10. Holy is Allah and His is the praise, Holy is Allah, the Most Great. Bless O Allah, Muḥammad and the people of Muḥammad.

this happens you will be the recipients of the blessings ofAllah the Exalted.

Triumph shall come only through prayers

This is the age of the latter-ones, with which Islam's triumphs is associated. We all know that these triumphs shall not come about with swords or guns or bombs, now the ultimate weapon is prayer, and then reasoning and arguments that have been given to the Promised Messiah[as]. It is through these indeed, *Inshā'Allāh*, that Islam is going to be triumphant. For the acceptance of prayer and to attain nearness to Allah and His blessings, He has told us in the verse mentioned earlier that blessings and salutations should be invoked on the Holy Prophet[sa], and we have understood from various Aḥādīth also that all this will not be possible without invoking blessings on the Holy Prophet[sa]. The Promised Messiah[as] has also told us that the station that has been granted to him has been granted due to (his) reciting *Durūd,* and it also has a unique connection with the future triumphs of Islam.

While mentioning his status through which Allah the Exalted sent him into the world as the Messiah and Mahdi, the Promised Messiah[as] mentions a revelation of his and says:

صَلِّ عَلٰی مُحَمَّدٍ وَّ اٰلِ مُحَمَّدٍ سَیِّدِ وُلْدِ اٰدَمَ خَاتَمِ النَّبِیِّیْن

Send blessings and salutations on Muḥammad, and on the people of Muḥammad who is the chief of the sons of Adam and is the Seal of the Prophets, may peace and blessings of Allah be upon him.

This indicates to the fact that all these dignities and beneficences and favours are only by means of him[sa] and are a reward for loving him[sa]. Glory to Allah, what lofty stations are there in the most eminent union with this chief of all creation and what kind of proximity it is that the one who loves him becomes Allah's beloved and the world becomes the servant of his servant. I am reminded here that one night this humble one invoked blessing on the Holy Prophet[sa] to such a degree that my heart and soul filled with its fragrance. That night I saw in my dream that (angels) were bringing water skins full of light into my house and one of them said to me, 'These are the blessings that you invoked on Muḥammad[sa]'.

.... Another similar wondrous incident comes to mind that once [I] had a revelation the meanings of which were that the higher angels are in commotion. That is, the Will of God is aroused to revive the faith. To bring faith back to life from anew. However, the appointment of the one who will bestow life to the dead, the *'Revivalist',* has not yet been revealed to the higher angels. It is not clear who is going to bring it back to life. That is the reason why there is conflict. At that moment, I saw in dream that people are looking around for a *'Revivalist'* and a person comes in front of this humble person and said while signalling (towards me):

هٰذَا رَجُلٌ يُّحِبُّ رَسُوْلَ اللّٰهِ

that is, this is the man who loves the Prophet of God and the meanings of these words were that the highest condition of this office is the love of the Prophet and that is certainly verified in this person.

Similarly the commandment to invoke blessings on thepeople of the Prophet[sa] in the above mentioned revelation has the same mystery; that love for the *Ahl-e-Bait* has a most elevated link with the diffusion of Divine luminosity. The person who joins the kindred of this most eminent union attains the legacy of these chaste and pure ones and is conferred with all their knowledge and spiritual discernment.

(Barāhīn-e-Aḥmadiyyah, Four parts, Sub-footnote #3, Rūḥānī Khazā'in Vol. 1, pp. 597-598)

The only way to restore the lost glory of Islam is to make an effort, after entering the fold of the community of the Promised Messiah[as]

Today, the revival of faith, the resurgence of the lost glory of Islam is by following the gallant of Allah whom Allah the Exalted established in the defence of the Holy Prophet[sa]. It is by following the reasoning and arguments taught by him that were told to him by Allah the Exalted and by fully implementing his teachings that the banner of Islam and the Holy Prophet[sa] will rise with its full glory and dignity, *Inshā'Allāh*, and shall continue to flourish.

The summary of what the Promised Messiah[as] says about the significance of this era and drawing the attention of people to it, is that Islam is undergoing hard times and for this reason Allah the Exalted established a mission that would restore the lost greatness. For this reason he said to the Muslims to give up their obstinacy and contemplate over the fact that would Allah the Exalted not be aroused to establish the honour of the Holy Prophet[sa] even in these circumstances when he[sa] is being attacked from all directions? Whereas, He invokes blessings and salutations on him.

The full extract is as follows:

> How blessed is this era that merely with His Grace, Allah the Exalted has willed the blessed objective for the manifestation of the greatness of the Holy Prophet[sa] during these tumultuous days; has arranged for the triumph of Islam from the Divine and established a mission. I would like to ask those people who have compassion for Islam and who have respect and consideration for it in their hearts that can they say if there has been a time worse than this in which this much abuse and disrespect of the Holy Prophet[sa] has taken place and the Holy Qur'an has been so blasphemed? I am then deeply saddened and distressed by the condition of the Muslims and at times I get anxious with this grief that there remains not even enough feeling in them to sense this disgrace. Did Allah the Exalted not regard any honour for the Holy Prophet[sa] in that would He

not have established a Divine mission on this extent of abuse to silence these opponents of Islam and to spread his[sa] greatness and purity in the world. In the event that Allah the Exalted and His angels invoke blessings and salutations on the Holy Prophet[sa], how essential it is to manifest these salutations at this time of abuse and Allah the Exalted has manifested this in the shape of this mission.

(Malfūẓāt Vol. 3 pp. 8- 9, New Edition)

Notice this phrase and how great a responsibility lies on the Aḥmadiyya Muslim Community who associate themselves with the Promised Messiah[as].

At a time when there is an ongoing furor against the Holy Prophet[sa], most certainly Allah the Exalted and His angels would be sending blessings and salutations on the Holy Prophet[sa], are indeed sending it. It is also our task, those who have attached themselves to the mission and the Community of the true and ardent devotee of the Holy Prophet[sa] and the Imam of the age, to mould our prayers in *Durūd* and infuse so much *Durūd* in the atmosphere with the sincerity of the heart that each particle of the atmosphere is fragrant with it and all our prayers gain acceptance in Allah's Presence by means of *Durūd*. This is the kind of demonstration of love that we should have for the person of the Holy Prophet[sa] and his people. May Allah also grant the Muslim *ummah* wisdom and sense to recognise this Messenger of Allah and to join the Community of the spiritual son of the Holy Prophet[sa], who are once again elevating the station of the Holy Prophet[sa] by creating an atmosphere of peace and love in the world. May Allah give these people the wisdom to see that despite being linked to the Holy Prophet[sa] today once again, 1,400 years later, in the very same month of *Muḥarram*, in the very same land, a Muslim is spilling the blood of a Muslim. However, the lesson has never been learned and they are continuing to spill blood. May Allah give them sense that they may desist from these actions and may they inculcate fear of God in their hearts, and may they follow the true teaching of Islam. All that they are currently involved in is because of not accepting the Imam of the age, and for disobeying the directive of the Holy Prophet[sa]. It is the responsibility of each Aḥmadī, and it is a huge responsibility indeed, for one who has accepted the Imam of the age to abundantly invoke *Durūd* for the love of the Prophet[sa], for your own sake, and for the sake of the other Muslims so that Allah may save the Muslim *ummah* from destruction.

It is the requisite of the love of the Holy Prophet[sa] that we generously include the Muslim *ummah* in our prayers. The intentions of the others (enemies) are also not right. Who knows what more trouble and turmoil these people are going to be entangled in, and these Muslims have to face it all, and what plans are being hatched against them. May Allah have mercy.

May Allah guide us on the right path, may we be grateful servants of God, may we be grateful to Him that He has enabled us to accept the Imam of the age, and now may He continue to enable us to honour this acceptance, and always keep us on the paths of His pleasure.

(4)

Friday Sermon Delivered on 3rd March, 2006 at Baitul Futūh Mosque, Morden, London, UK

****

(4)

Friday Sermon Delivered on 3rd March, 2006

- The allegations that the Promised Messiah[as] has abolished Jihad, changed Islamic commandments and teachings of the Holy Prophet[sa], and with his coming the era of the Holy Prophet[sa] has ended, are absolutely false, cruel, and nefarious.

- By the Grace of God, our hearts are filled with thousands, rather, millions times more with the love of the Holy Prophet[sa] than the hearts of those who fabricate such baseless and nefarious allegations against us.

- Publication of a baseless and far fetched news about Jamā'at Aḥmadiyya in the daily *'Jang'* while quoting publication of the defaming caricatures of the Holy Prophet[sa] in a Danish newspaper is nothing but a mischievous and provocative act.

- I say to the fabricator of the false news, "It is certainly a big lie, and I invoke the curse of Allah on liars by saying: li: *la'natullāhi 'alal kādhibīn."*

****

اَشْهَدُ اَنْ لاَّ اِلٰهَ اِلاَّ اللّٰهُ وَحْدَهٗ لاَ شَرِيْكَ لَهٗ وَ اَ شْهَدُ اَنَّ مُحَمَّدًا عَبْدُهٗ وَرَسُوْلُهٗ .

اَمَّا بَعْدُ فَاَعُوْذُ بِاللّٰهِ مِنَ الشَّيْطٰنِ الرَّجِيْمِ

بِسْمِ اللّٰهِ الرَّحْمٰنِ الرَّحِيْمِ 0

اَلْحَمْدُ لِلّٰهِ رَبِّ الْعٰلَمِيْنَ 0 الرَّحْمٰنِ الرَّحِيْمِ 0 مٰلِكِ يَوْمِ الدِّيْنِ 0 اِيَّاكَ نَعْبُدُ وَاِيَّاكَ نَسْتَعِيْنُ 0 اِهْدِنَا الصِّرَاطَ الْمُسْتَقِيْمَ 0 صِرَاطَ الَّذِيْنَ اَنْعَمْتَ عَلَيْهِمْ ۙ غَيْرِ الْمَغْضُوْبِ عَلَيْهِمْ وَلاَ الضَّآلِّيْنَ0

I bear witness that there is none worthy of worship except Allāh and He is One and has no partner. And I bear witness that Muḥammad is His Servant and Messenger.

After this, I seek refuge with Allah from Satan, the rejected

In the Name of Allah, the Gracious, the Merciful

All praise belongs to Allah, Lord of all the worlds. The Gracious, the Merciful. Master of the Day of Judgment. Thee alone do we worship and Thee alone do we implore for help. Guide us in the right path -- The path of those on whom Thou has bestowed *Thy* blessings, those who have not incurred displeasure, and those who have not gone astray. (Sūrah Al-Fātiḥah, 1:1-7)

Publication of the false and baseless news in the newspaper, the *'Jang'* (London), is a provocative and mischievous act

Yesterday, the London edition of the newspaper, *'Jang',* published a certain news item, which is not even remotely connected to the beliefs of the Aḥmadiyya Muslim Community. This has been published solely to create mischief. It is not only against our beliefs, the incident it refers to also is not true. It did not ever take place. This news item has perhaps also been printed in Pakistan, etc, as well. If not yesterday, it would have been printed by today. These newspapers are very swift in printing such news items to increase their sales. They have developed the habit of committing crude improprieties, and printing utter fabrications to increase their circulation. We are all too aware of their Pakistan edition in that it speaks nonsense and untruths about us every now and then.

A wave of extreme indignation has been generated among the Muslims because of the recent publication of absurd and outrageous caricatures in Danish newspapers, which were later reproduced in newspapers of other countries. Due to this, the Muslims are feeling severe indignation. Strike actions are being taken, and rallies are being carried out. Anyway when there is no one to watch over how anger is expressed, and no one to stem the flow of it and to give it the right direction then such reactions materialise. No matter what sort of a Muslim one is, whether or not regular in Prayers, whether or not abiding by the commandments, but when the reputation of the Prophet[sa] is at stake his sense of honour is aroused, and he is prepared to give his life for it. To publish this news under such circumstances, and that too on a Thursday, when today, Friday, many places are planning to take out rallies, to take strike actions and similar other reactions has been done solely to create an atmosphere against the Aḥmadīs. It is a most cruel and seditious attempt to use this news item to incite the uninformed Muslims to target the Aḥmadīs with oppression. Anyhow, they always try not to let go away any opportunity to arouse the uninformed Muslims against the Aḥmadīs.

Many among you would have read this news item, however, as everyone does not read it, I shall read the news item.

The news item has been attributed to Dr. Jāved Kañwal who is the newspaper's reporter in Denmark.

He writes it as news from Copenhagen:

> On the condition of anonymity while discussing the issue of the caricatures, a responsible officer of the Danish secret service has told the Daily *'Jang'* that in September 2005, the Qādiānīs held their Annual Convention in Denmark which was attended by leading figures of the Qādiānīs. On this occasion, a delegation of the Qādiānīs met with a Danish Minister and while discussing Jihad, told him that they alone were the standard bearers of true Islamic teachings.

So far so good, although we have not specifically told them that but it is our claim indeed that the Aḥmadiyya Muslim Community is the standard bearer of the true teachings of Islam.

He goes on to write:

> Their Prophet, Mirzā Ghulām Aḥmad Qādianī had abrogated Jihad.

This is correct, but the abrogation was declared with conditions.

Then he writes:

> Mirzā Ghulām Aḥmad Qādianī has, God forbid, changed the Islamic commandments.

This is a baseless accusation and allegation. Note their mischief that follows.

He writes:

> This is because the teachings and the era of the Holy Prophet[sa] have come to an end, God forbid.

The newspaper further writes:

> On the assurance of the Qādiānīs that the followers of the Holy Prophet[sa] are only limited to Saudi Arabia, on 30th September 2005, the Danish newspaper published twelve

caricatures with reference to the Holy Prophet[sa]. The focal point of these was to attack the philosophy of Jihad. The high-level Danish officer said that they were certain as of the beginning of January that the Qādiānī claim was right because up till January no country other than Saudi Arabia had made a formal complaint to them. The silence from OIC confirmed their conviction. The responsible officer let our reporter listen to a video tape of this meeting with a recoding of the conversation in Danish, Urdu and English languages.

(Daily *'Jang'* London 2nd March 2006 pp. 1 and 3)

As if the conversation with him took place in three languages! Lies have no legs. It is a most outrageously baseless news item. Dr. Kañwal seems to be a very special correspondent of the newspaper, *'Jang'*. It was first thought that he was from Denmark but now it has transpired that he is from Italy and represents *'Jang'* and *'Geo'* from there. As far as I have gathered the information, legally he cannot give news with reference to Denmark to any newspaper.

The first thing is the accusation that the Community held a convention in September. Last year the Aḥmadiyya Muslim Community did not hold the Annual Convention there at all. Due to my visit, a combined Annual Convention of the Scandinavian countries was held and that too in Sweden. It was seen on MTA (Muslim Television Aḥmadiyya) by all as to what was said there and what was not said.

During my visit to Denmark, a reception was held in a hotel which was attended by some sections of the press and other well-informed friends. Some officials were also present there and a lady Minister had also come. The beautiful and peaceable teachings of Islam were mentioned there with reference to the Holy Qur'an, Aḥādīth, and discourses of the Promised Messiah[as]. Whatever was said there was clear and unambiguous. Nothing was said surreptitiously. The newspapers gave it coverage, in fact a little was also shown on the television. There was no separate meeting. It was just my speech at the reception which I think MTA has shown. If they have not, they may do so now. Anyway, it is true that maybe in that speech a mention was made of people like this writer, in that it is these few people who bring Islam in disrepute, otherwise the majority of Muslims disapprove of this sort of Jihad and terrorism.

Anyway a huge fabrication has been attributed to us that belie even the most habitual of liars, who would think twice before speaking up in that everything is on record these days. In fact according to this person a videotape exists in Urdu, English and Danish. If they are truthful they may show the tapes, show them to us as well, in this way it can be made clear who said what.

I say to the fabricator of this false news, "It is entirely a big lie, and I invoke the curse of Allah on liars by saying: *la'natullāhi 'alal kādhibīn.*"

Firstly I would say to those who have spread this false

news:

It is nothing but an absolute lie, and

لَعْنَةُ اللّٰهِ عَلَى الْكَاذِبِيْنَ

(The curse of Allah on those who lie)

If they are truthful, they may repeat the very same words. However, if they had an iota of fear of God they could never repeat these words. Generally, these people have a little fear of God, if any. However, even if they do not repeat these words still having spoken a lie of this great magnitude they have come under this prayer of the Promised Messiah[as]. In any case, such contemptible improprieties have been taking place against the Aḥmadiyya Muslim Community in the past, and continue to do so. Whenever they try to stab us in the back in their presumption, Allah the Exalted causes them to fail, and manifests His love for the Aḥmadiyya Muslim Community in a way that brings forth His enhanced Grace.

Jamā'at-e-Aḥmadiyya's efforts and reaction to the mischief of caricatures

Ever since this mischief of the caricatures began, the Aḥmadiyya Muslim Community was the first one to raise the issue, and had tried to stop the newspaper from doing it. I have already mentioned this. In addition, in December and January we again wrote to these newspapers, and clearly stated our feelings. In those days, I was in Qādiān when our Missionary wrote to the newspaper. Our Missionary's interview was published in the newspaper. This paper reported about the response of the Aḥmadiyya Muslim Community regarding this matter. After writing that these people prefer to present their lives moulded on the model of the Holy Prophet[sa] than to damage and destruction, he wrote that it does not mean that the Imam (it was Imam's interview) is not hurt by the caricatures. Rather, he is heart broken by the caricatures. In fact his pain and hurt inspired him to promptly write an article on the caricatures issue. Accordingly, this article was duly written and published in a Danish newspaper.

It is the love of the Promised Messiah[as] for the Holy Prophet[sa] that has so enthused the Community with such love that the European Christian converts to Aḥmadiyyat, the true Islam, are also steeped in it.

An interview of one of our Danish Aḥmadī Muslims, 'Abdus Salām Madsen was published in the newspaper *'Venster Bladet'* on 16th February 2006. It was a long interview, and I shall read out a part of it.

Its translation is:

> Mr. Madsen further said that the Prime Minister of Denmark should have talked with the Ambassadors of the Muslim countries, as seeing the caricatures makes people very angry. Had the Prime Minister of Denmark consulted with the Ambassadors of the Muslim countries he would have known how serious the matter was, and what consequences could ensue. The response that materialised is exactly the kind of reaction I felt would follow the publication of the caricatures. This is because the Holy Prophet[sa] is an exemplar for every Muslim in every aspect of life. When a contemptible attack is launched against such a person, it is distressing for every Muslim. They feel pain and hurt.
>
> Mr. 'Abdus Salām Madsen asks what did the Danish newspaper, *Yoland Posten,* achieve by publishing these caricatures? It is further reported that Mr. Madsen was also most distressed at the publication of the caricatures of the Holy Prophet[sa]. Then he writes that the description of the appearance of the Holy Prophet[sa] as to how his appearance was is well-documented. The fact is that this is simply a dirty and childish act.
>
> He further wrote that Denmark has an anti-defamation law. I used to think that it was not necessary but I now believe that to stem disorder it is required to apply this law. As far as the defamation of the Holy Prophet[sa] is concerned, the matter is with God and He shall chastise for it.

Observe, how solid faith a European Aḥmadī Muslim has!

Such were our reactions to this disgusting act concerning the Holy Prophet[sa].

Promised Messiah's[as] love of the Holy Prophet[sa]

By the Grace of God our hearts are filled with love of the Holy Prophet[sa], a million times more than the people who levy such accusations and allegations against us. All this is due to the beautiful teachings of the Holy Prophet[sa] instilled in our hearts, which is illustrated by the Promised Messiah[as], and which he has beautified for us. No Aḥmadī can ever even contemplate that, God forbid, the station of the Promised Messiah[as] is greater than that of the Holy Prophet[sa]. The depth and intensity of the Promised Messiah's[as] love for the Holy Prophet[sa] was such that he would be moved to tears by a poetical verse said by Ḥaḍrat Ḥassān bin Thābit[ra]. The poetical verse is:

كُنْتَ السَّوَادَ لِنَاظِرِيْ فَعَمِيَ عَلَيْكَ النَّاظِر

مَنْ شَآءَ بَعْدَكَ فَلْيَمُتْ فَعَلَيْكَ كُنْتُ اُحَاذِر

O Muḥammad[sa], you were [like] the pupil of my eye that I am blinded of today. Whosoever may die now, I feared your death alone.

(Dīwān Ḥassān bin Thābit)

The Promised Messiah[as] would wish that if only it had been him who had said this poetic verse. It is grossly criminal to allege about a person such as him that he, God forbid, considered himself greater than the Holy Prophet[sa] or that his adherents give him a higher status than the Holy Prophet[sa]. We see examples, at each step, of his enthralling love for the Holy Prophet[sa]. In a poetic verse he says:

اس نورپر فدا ھوں اس کا ھی میں ھوا ھوں
وہ ھے میں چیز کیا ھوں بس فیصلہ یھی ھے

I am totally devoted to that luminosity and to him alone do I belong
He is the one who counts; while I amount to naught, this alone is the final word.

(Qādiān kay Āryah aur Hamm, Rūḥānī Khazā'in, Vol. 20, p. 456)

To say about the one who is so utterly devoted to this luminosity that, God forbid, he claims that the status of the Holy Prophet[sa] is not the same any more and the station of Mirzā Ghulām Aḥmad Qādiānī has been elevated, and the Aḥmadīs consider Mirzā Ghulām Aḥmad Qādiānī as the last

Prophet, and that we told them that this is our belief that he is the last Prophet, and we give the newspaper a free hand, God forbid, to make caricatures of the Holy Prophet[sa]. About this all I can say:

اِنَّا لِلّٰهِ وَاِنَّآ اِلَيْهِ رٰجِعُوْنَ

and

لَعْنَةُ اللّٰهِ عَلَى الْكَاذِبِيْنَ

It is extremely childish thinking that the newspaper was only awaiting for our permission to print those caricatures, whereas, we are just a few hundreds in Denmark. Before printing news, this Urdu newspaper should reflect a little about the pros and cons.

Muslim Governments should not succumb to the cunning plans of the selfish mullāhs and other elements

The Danish government is perhaps not so far gone, however, those who wrote this news item and those who printed it seem totally devoid of sensibility. There is nothing in their minds but mischief. There seems to be no other reason for printing this news item than to incite the Muslims. They are aware that Muslims are aroused by this name. So they wanted to create turmoil in countries where anti-Aḥmadiyya feelings are high, such as, Bangladesh, Indonesia, and Pakistan. It would not be far-fetched that certain elements might have started the movement with the ulterior motive of starting movements against the governments of these countries. We have noticed that up till now whenever a movement against Aḥmadīs was started it ended up as ananti-government movement. Therefore, these governments should have some common sense and should not be taken in one by the opportunist *mullāhs* or other such elements. As far as the station of the Holy Prophet[sa] is concerned, in our eyes, one might have seen and judged it from the poetic verses of the Promised Messiah[as] that I just read. Each Aḥmadī knows the status he has in their heart for the Holy Prophet[sa]. I have mentioned this in my previous sermons. I have given sermons on this topic. We have expressed our pain, and continue to express it. Statements of protest by us have been printed all over the world. We have also issued press releases. We did not make all these statements for ostentatious purposes or for the sake of someone else or with the fear of the Muslims. Rather, this is part of our faith. Our existence is of no value without the connection to the Holy Prophet[sa]. I shall read some extracts of the Promised Messiah[as] in this regard to further expound on the matter.

The gist of the teachings of the Promised Messiah[as]

He[as] states:

The summary and the crux of our religion is,

لَآ اِلٰهَ اِلاَّ اللّٰهُ مُحَمَّدٌ رَّسُوْلُ اللّٰهِ [11]

Our belief, which we hold in this life here on earth and to which we will continue to adhere firmly till the time that we pass on to the next world, is that our spiritual leader and master, Muḥammad[sa] is the Seal of the Prophets and the Best of the Messengers. At his hands religion has been perfected and blessings of Allah have been consummated which lead man to the right path and further on to Himself.

(Izāla-e-Auhām, Rūḥānī Khazāi'n, Vol. 3, pp. 169-170)

So this is what constitutes our faith, and these are the teachings given to us by the Promised Messiah[as]. How could it ever be said about the one who has this faith that he could reach Allah the Exalted or was granted prophethood without his mediation?

He further states:

The right path is only the religion of Islam. Now there is only one Prophet and only one Book under the heavens. The Prophet is Ḥaḍrat Muḥammad[sa], the chosen one, who is higher and more exalted than all the Prophets and is the most perfect of all Messengers and is the

11. There is none worthy of worship but Allah, Muḥammad is the Messenger of Allah

> *'Khātam-ul-Anbiyā"*, and the best of men. By following him, God Almighty is found, all the veils of deep darkness are lifted, and signs of true salvation are witnessed in this very life. The Book is theHoly Qur'an, which comprises true and perfect guidanceand effectiveness. Through which knowledge and understanding of the Divine are obtained, the heart is purified of human weaknesses, and after getting delivered from ignorance, heedlessness and doubts, a personarrives at the stage of complete certainty.
>
> (Brāhīn-e-Aḥmadiyya, Four parts, part 4, Sub-footnote 3, Rūḥānī Khazā'in, Vol. 1, pp. 557-558)

That is, all that can now be attained will be attained through the Holy Prophet[sa]. Prophethood was perfected through him and it is through his teachings that darkness can be dispelled and enlightenment attained. Nearness to God is also reached through him as well as true salvation, and the impurities of the heart will be cleansed with the teachings that the Holy Prophet[sa] brought.

He[as] further states:

> Our Holy Prophet[sa] was a great reformer for the proclamation of truth, and restored to the world the truth that had been lost. No Prophet shares with him the pride that he found the entire world in darkness and by his advent that darkness was converted into light. He did not die till the people among whom he had appeared had cast aside the garment of *shirk* and had put on the robe of *Tauḥīd*. Not only this, but also they achieved high grades of faith and performed such works of righteousness,

fidelity and certainty which are not matched in any part of the world. Such success was not achieved by any Prophet other than the Holy Prophet[sa]. It is a strong argument in support of the truth of the Holy Prophet[sa] that he was raised in an age when the world had fallen into deep darkness and called for a grand Reformer. He departed the world at a time when hundreds of thousands of people had abandoned *shirk* and idol worship and had adopted *Tauḥīd* and the straight path. Such perfect reformation was exclusive to him. He taught a people, who were at the level of animals, the ways of humanity.

He taught manners of civility to a people who were wild, living like animals.

In other words, he converted wild beasts into men, i.e., he turned animals into human beings. Then he turned them into educated men, made them men of God, breathed spirituality into them, and created a relationship between them and the True God. They were slaughtered like sheep in the cause of God and were trodden under foot like ants, but they did not abandon their faith, and marched forward in the face of every calamity. Undoubtedly, our Holy Prophet[sa] was a second Adam, and indeed he was the true Adam for the establishment of spirituality through whom all human excellences arrived at their perfection, and all good faculties were devoted to their proper task and no branch of human nature was left barren. Prophethood ended with him not only because he was the last Prophet in a point of time, but also because all the excellences of prophethood reached their climax in him. As he was a perfect manifestation of Divine attributes, his *Sharia* had the qualities of both majesty and of beauty. That is why he

> was named Muḥammad and Aḥmad[sa]. And there was no miserliness in his prophethood; indeed, it was destined for the benefit of the entire world since the beginning of time.
>
> (Lecture Siālkot, Rūḥānī Khazā'in. Vol. 20, pp. 206, 207)

This is the teaching of the Aḥmadiyya Muslim Jamā'at that the beneficence of the Holy Prophet[sa] continues till today.

He further states:

> The Holy Prophet[sa] is *'Khātamun-Nabiyyīn'*, that is, after the Holy Prophet[sa] there will be no other *Sharia*, no new Book and no new commandments.

And they say that a new *Sharia* has been introduced and that we consider Mirzā Ghulām Aḥmad greater than the Holy Prophet!!

> This Book and these teachings shall be enduring. The words of 'Prophet' and 'Messenger' in my book[s] regarding me most certainly are not suggestive that a new *Sharia* or new commandments will be taught. Rather, the objective is that when Allah the Exalted appoints someone at the time of true need, He grants him the honour of Divine dialogue.

Meaning that He speaks to him.

> He gives him information of the unseen and this is where the word Prophet is applicable to him.

The word Prophet is used for one with whom Allah the Exalted speaks abundantly.

> And the appointed one is given the title of *Nabī*. It does not mean that he brings a new *Sharia* or that he, God forbid, cancels the *Sharia* of the Holy Prophet[sa].

They are making a false allegation against us.

> Whatever he is given, is granted only through sincere and absolute obedience to the Holy Prophet[sa], and it cannot be achieved without it.

(Al-Ḥakam, 10th January 1904, p. 2)

So, when the claimant himself says in decisive words that I am attaining everything through him and nothing can be achieved without him, and his followers are also firm on the belief that he is the true and ardent devotee of the Holy Prophet[sa], then the purpose of the talks, which are based on falsehood and lies is nothing but to create confusion among the Muslims. People always have been doing so. Apart from creating chaos, these satanic forces are ever seething with jealousy in that they cannot bear the progress of the Community, it bothers them considerably. They may resort to as many distasteful acts, as they have done in the past, and will perhaps continue in the future, people of this ilk will continue to be around. Satan has to keep going. *Inshā'Allāh*, our progress will not be hindered by their disgraceful deeds.

The grand status of the Holy Prophet[sa] in the sight of the Promised Messiah[as]

The Promised Messiah[as] further states about the status of the Holy Prophet[sa]: Vital

> The sublime light which was bestowed on man, i.e., the most perfect among them, was not shared by angels, nor by stars; nor was it in the moon, nor in the sun, or in the oceans and the rivers. It was not to be found in rubies or emeralds, nor in sapphires, nor in pearls. It was not in any earthly or heavenly object.

That is, it was neither in an earthly matter nor in the Heaven.

> It was possessed only by the perfect man, manifested in the most consummate way in the person of our lord and master, Muḥammad, the chosen one[sa], the chief of all Prophets, leader of those who live (in the sight of Allah). So, that light was bestowed on that man and likewise, to a degree, on all who in their several ways were similar to him.

His followers were given the light in accordance to their faith.

> Trust denotes all the faculties of the perfect man, his wisdom, knowledge, life and soul, senses, fears, love, honour, dignity and all collective blessings both physical and spiritual, which Allah the Exalted bestowed on the perfect man.

It means that all of man's abilities of wisdom, knowledge and other senses, the highest of strengths and the highest of standards of these, were given to the perfect man.

The perfect man, in accordance with the verse:

اِنَّ اللّٰهَ يَاْمُرُكُمْ اَنْ تُؤَدُّوا الْاَمٰنٰتِ اِلٰٓى اَهْلِهَا[12]

returns all this trust to God Almighty, i.e., by fully submersing himself in Him he devotes himself to His cause .....

This glory was found in its highest, most perfect form in our lord and master, our guide, the unlettered Prophet[sa], the truthful and the one whom the truthful verified, Muḥammad, the chosen one[sa].

(Ā'īna-e-Kamālāt-e-Islam, Rūḥānī Khazā'in. Vol. 5, pp 160-162)

So these people, who consider themselves as devotee of the Holy Prophet[sa], and accuse us that, God forbid, we consider the Promised Messiah[as] greater than him, their sole objectives are to gain their personal benefits. If only they could demonstrate that anyone of their religious scholars could exhibit such glorious, or even a minuscule quantity of such glorious eloquence about the Holy Prophet[sa] as the Promised Messiah[as] has expressed! These are the words of a

12. Verily, Allah commands you to make over the trusts to those entitled to them. (Sūrah Al-Nisā', 4:59)

sincere, and ardent devotee about the Holy Prophet[sa], whom they call a liar. Everything he did or avoided doing was in obedience to his lord and master Ḥaḍrat Muḥammad[sa]. Let us see if this depth of eloquence and this profound a perception of the person of the Holy Prophet[sa] is in your literature, as it has been presented by the Promised Messiah[as].

The Promised Messiah[as] further states - and this has always been the teaching of the Community, we abide by it, we tolerate it all, staying within the law.

He stated:

> This indeed is the summary of our religion. How could we reconcile with those who unfairly and without fear of God address our esteemed Holy Prophet[sa] with foul language, make wicked false allegations against his holy person, and do not abstain from being abusive? I say most truthfully that we could reconcile with the most poisonous of snakes, and with wild wolves but we could not reconcile with these people who make vulgar attacks on our beloved Prophet[sa] who is dearer to us than our lives and our parents. May God bring death upon us while we are Muslim. We do not want to do something that would compromise faith.
>
> (Paighām-e-Ṣulaḥ, Rūḥānī Khazā'in, Vol. 23, p. 459)

So this is our teaching. This is the teaching, which has been given to us by the Promised Messiah[as]. This is the fire of the ardent love and devotion for the Holy Prophet[sa] that the

Promised Messiah[as] kindled in our hearts and gave us its correct understanding and perception. If after all this, they still say that, God forbid, the Aḥmadiyya Community encouraged the Danish government and the newspaper to publish the caricatures, and it was after this that they printed the caricatures, then the only thing we can do with these people is to send the curse of Allah the Exalted on them.

The reality of the issue of *"Jihad with the Sword"*

The other matter is about the abrogation of Jihad. This is the first thing the correspondent wrote, however, the significant point he raised was that we, God forbid, do not believe in the Holy Prophet[sa] as a Prophet or that now his teaching is abolished. The other issue he raised was that of the abrogation of Jihad. With respect to this, the Muslim leaders who have been put on the spot under the pressure of the powers of whom they are toadies, and whom they scrounge, have given statements that the Jihad as defined today, and the frequent acts of certain Muslim organisations is not Jihad. It is totally against the teachings of Islam. Their statements have been printed in the newspapers. This has been the stance of the Aḥmadiyya Muslim Community from the very start. This is our ideology and this is our teaching that in the current age, under these circumstances, Jihad is abolished, and this is exactly in accordance with the Islamic teachings.

The Promised Messiah[as] says about this matter:

> The battles of our Prophet[sa] and those of his esteemed Companions[ra] were either in defence of the attack by the non-Muslims or to maintain peace and to push back those by the sword who wanted to stop faith by the sword. However, who among the opponents, now picks up the sword to defend the faith? Who prevents one from becoming a Muslim, and who forbids calling the *Adhān* in mosques?
>
> (Tiryāqul-Qulūb, Rūḥānī Khazā'in, Vol. 15, pp. 159-160)

That is who forbids calling the *Adhān*? It is only in Pakistan that the Aḥmadīs are forbidden to call the *Adhān* in mosques but we are silent despite this. We did not make a commotion, and we offer our Prayers without calling the *Adhān*.

He[as] further states:

> There is a clear Hadith[13] in *Bukhārī,* which points to the glory of the Promised Messiah[as] [14] يَضَعُ الْحَرْبَ That is, the Promised Messiah[as] will not fight.
>
> How astonishing it is that on one hand they maintain that after the Holy Qur'an, *Ṣaḥiḥ Bukhārī* is the most authentic

13. (Ṣaḥīḥ Bukhārī, Kitāb-ul-Anbiyā', Bābu Nuzūlin 'Īsabni Maryam)
14. He will do away with war.

book, and on the other hand they base their beliefs on other Aḥādīth, which are clearly contrary to the Hadith of *Bukhārī.*

(Tiryāqul Qulūb, Rūḥānī Khazā'in, Vol. 15, p. 159)

Thus, this is the ideology of the Aḥmadiyya Muslim Community, which is in accordance to the Holy Qur'an and Hadith. We announce with a drumbeat and say, in fact we have always been saying, that what is being masqueraded as Jihad by these people in this day and age, is nothing but terrorism. It is not Jihad and is totally against the teachings of Islam.

Just yesterday, a suicide bombing took place in Karachi. People like these bring Islam in disrepute. With these attacks they kill innocent people of their own country. It is they who by doing such improper activities are refuting Islam and the teachings of the Holy Prophet[sa], whereas, the Aḥmadīs are engaged in the Jihad of taking the message of the Holy Prophet[sa] to the world. Who among these people is taking the message of Islam to the corners of the world in this manner? Certainly, the Aḥmadīs who never before have participated in your terrorist activities, and Jihadī efforts that bring Islam in disrepute, will not do so in the future. In any case, these are just the contemptible efforts to disgrace the Aḥmadiyya Community that have always taken place.

There will be a full inquiry of the false news and the disgusting conspiracy so that the real aims could be elicited

I tell to the newspaper also that they should be mindful that Denmark is not a country where there is no rule of law; unlike Pakistan, where if the *mullāh* so wishes only then the law is enforced and where no justice is done. Anyhow, these people have some sense of justice. We are collecting all the facts, and have asked for reports to be sent in. By printing the news with reference to a Danish officer and maintaining that the caricatures were published on the assurance of the Aḥmadiyya Community in that, God forbid, the teaching of the Holy Prophet[sa] has been canceled, they are alleging that the Danish government was also embroiled in this. Meanwhile, the Danish Prime Minister has been vociferous and has given many statements that the action was taken by the newspaper and that they disapproved of it but could not say anything due to the freedom of the press. Exactly what is freedom of press is a completely separate issue. Anyway, they deny it, while the newspaper maintains that their government is involved. Therefore the Danish government also reserves the right to take action against this news item. In the current climate, with the wave of anger spread across the Muslim world against Denmark, publishing this fabricated news item with their reference is like inflaming the situation further. We have been in touch with them. The officer of the Secret Service of Denmark has clearly denied this and has refuted that this ever took place or that they had any information about this. They have said that they will carry out further investigation, which will make things clearer. It was first published in the newspaper [*Jang*] that they had a video tape of the event, when we contacted them, they changed their minds and said that they did not have a video tape but an audio tape is available. As I said falsehood has no legs. They will keep changing their statements and such is the characteristic of Pakistani journalism or journalism that has Pakistani influence.

Anyhow, let me make it clear that this matter will not end here. This disgusting allegation against us, which is an effort to conspire against the Aḥmadīs in the current climate, we shall, therefore, take this matter as far as the law of the land will allow, and *Inshā'Allāh* will take it to its conclusion. So that the moral values of these so-called educated people may be exposed to the Muslims, at least to those Muslims who are decent-natured people. As I said earlier, disgusting allegations have always been made against us, but we have always exercised patience and have ever kept this directive, this teaching, of the Promised Messiah[as] in view:

He[as] states:

> I know very well that whatever we and our Community are, we will have the help and assistance of Allah the Exalted in the event that we stay on the straight path and carry out complete and perfect obedience to the Holy Prophet[sa]; [that we] make the teachings of the Holy Qur'an our *modus operandi* and that we verify these matters with our actions and demeanour, not with mere words. If we adopt this approach, then remember that most certainly, even if the whole world together wishes to destroy us, we

will not be destroyed, because God will be with us. *Inshā 'Allāh.*

(Al-Ḥakam, 24th September, 1904, p. 4)

May Allah always enable us to act according to this advice and may Allah always be with us and may He make these wicked people a lesson for others.

(5)

Friday Sermon Delivered on 10th March, 2006 at Baitul Futūh Mosque, Morden, London, UK

****

(5)

Friday Sermon Delivered on 10th March, 2006

- Today's Jihadist organizations, without any valid reasons and without any lawful authority through their warmongering slogans and actions have given the non-Muslims an opportunity to make foul attacks so daringly and shamelessly against the blessed personality of the Holy Prophet[sa].

- The Holy Prophet[sa] was an embodiment of mercy. He was blessed with a heart which fulfilled such high standards and demands of mercy, which no one else can do.

- Some of the beautiful incidents regarding freedom of conscience, freedom of religion and religious tolerance from the blessed life of the Holy Prophet[sa].

****

اَشْهَدُ اَنْ لَّآ اِلٰهَ اِلاَّ اللّٰهُ وَحْدَہٗ لاَ شَرِيْكَ لَهٗ وَ اَشْهَدُ اَنَّ مُحَمَّدًا عَبْدُهٗ وَرَسُوْلُهٗ .

اَمَّا بَعْدُ فَاَعُوْذُ بِاللّٰهِ مِنَ الشَّيْطٰنِ الرَّجِيْمِ

بِسْمِ اللّٰهِ الرَّحْمٰنِ الرَّحِيْمِ ۝

اَلْحَمْدُ لِلّٰهِ رَبِّ الْعٰلَمِيْنَ ۝ الرَّحْمٰنِ الرَّحِيْمِ ۝ مٰلِكِ يَوْمِ الدِّيْنِ ۝ اِيَّاكَ نَعْبُدُ وَاِيَّاكَ نَسْتَعِيْنُ ۝ اِهْدِنَا الصِّرَاطَ الْمُسْتَقِيْمَ ۝ صِرَاطَ الَّذِيْنَ اَنْعَمْتَ عَلَيْهِمْ ۝ غَيْرِ الْمَغْضُوْبِ عَلَيْهِمْ وَلاَ الضَّآلِّيْنَ ۝

I bear witness that there is none worthy of worship except Allah and He is One and has no partner. And I bear witness that Muḥammad is His Servant and Messenger.

After this, I seek refuge with Allah from Satan, the rejected

In the Name of Allah, the Gracious, the Merciful

All praise belongs to Allah, Lord of all the worlds. The Gracious, the Merciful. Master of the Day of Judgment. Thee alone do we worship and Thee alone do we implore for help. Guide us in the right path -- The path of those on whom Thou has bestowed *Thy* blessings, those who have not incurred displeasure, and those who have not gone astray. (Sūrah Al-Fātiḥah, 1:1-7)

Anti-Islamic activities of certain Muslim groups help non-Muslims in their attacks against Islam

I have spoken many times before concerning the objections raised by the non-Muslims with respect to the personality of the Holy Prophet[sa], that he, God forbid, brought a religion, which entails nothing but harshness, killing and destruction, that in Islam there is no concept of religious tolerance, restraint or freedom. That it is the effect of this teaching that have today become a part of the psyche of the Muslims. In this regard, I have stated many times before that, unfortunately, it is certain sects and groups within Muslims who are the cause of generating and establishing this concept. Unfortunately, it is the enactment of this ideology that has created the opportunity for the non-Muslim world, in particular the West, to exhibit absurd, extremely foul and depraved thoughts about our beloved master the Holy Prophet[sa]. Whereas, we know that the actions of these certain sects and groups are totally against the Islamic teachings and the code of conduct. The teachings of Islam are so beautiful that any unbiased person could not fail to be influenced by their beauty.

Beautiful teachings of Islam with regard to good treatment of non-Muslims

The Holy Qur'an repeatedly mentions beautiful teachings of Islam pertaining to good conduct with the non-Muslims, the safeguarding of their rights, fairness and justice with them, freedom of their religion, and no coercion in matters of faith, etc. There are many such directives relating to both Muslims and non-Muslims. Indeed, fighting is also permitted in certain situations. It is permitted only in the event that the enemy initiates (a fight), breaches pacts, is brutally unjust or oppressive. Even in these circumstances, no group or party of a country has the right, rather, it is up to the government to decide what to do and how to end the oppression. It is not up to any and every Jihādī organisation to rise, and to take up the task.

Exemplary good behaviour of the Holy Prophet[sa] compared to the excesses and tyranny of the infidels of Mecca and the enemies of Islam

At the time of the Holy Prophet[sa], specific situations were created for wars, which left Muslims with no choice but to fight back in defence. However, as I said, the current-day Jihadī organizations, with their militant slogans and actions, without having any warrantable reasons and rightful authority, have given others the opportunity, and courage to become audacious and shameless enough to make nonsensical attacks on the holy person of the Holy Prophet[sa], and continue doing so. Whereas, the Holy Prophet[sa] was the personification of compassion; a benefactor for humanity and a great defender of human rights who would not miss a chance to facilitate the enemy even at the time of a battle. Each step of his life, his each deed, in fact each moment of his life is a testimony to the fact that he was an embodiment of compassion with a heart that surpassed all others in fulfilling the requisites of compassion and kindness. He did so at the time of peace, at war, at home, outside the home, in his daily routine as well as in honouring the pacts with people of other religions. He established high standards of freedom of conscience and freedom of religion and tolerance. When he entered Mecca as the great conqueror, he granted amnesty to the conquered people and gave them total freedom of religion. Thus, he established an excellent example of the Qur'añic injunction:

لَآ اِكْرَاهَ فِى الدِّيْنِ قف

There should be no compulsion in religion. (Sūrah Al-Baqarah, 2:257)

Religion is a matter of an individual's heart and mind. He only desired that they accepted the true religion and thus made their life better both here and in the Hereafter, and tried to achieve forgiveness for themselves. However, there is no compulsion. His life is replete with similar illuminating examples of tolerance, freedom of religion and conscience, of which I shall mention a few now.

The hardship and pain of the thirteen year period in

Mecca after his claim of prophethood is known to all. The Prophet[sa] and his Companions[ra] endured great suffering and torment. They were laid on the scorching midday sand while hot stones were placed on their chests. They were flogged. Women were killed by having their legs torn apart. They were martyred. A range of tortures were inflicted on the Prophet[sa] himself. At times the innards of a camel were placed on his back while he was prostrating, which would make it impossible for him to get up. During his visit to *Ṭā'if* children threw stones at him, hurled abuse at him. Their leaders kept on inciting them. His injuries made him bleed profusely from head, and his shoes were filled with blood. Then there is the incident of *Sha'b Abī Ṭālib* when he, his family and his followers were held under siege for many years. They had nothing to eat or drink, and children starved. A Companion felt something soft under his feet at night which he picked up and put in his mouth, imagining it to be food. Such was their desperation due to hunger. Eventually, compelled by these circumstances, the migration to Medīna took place; the enemy did not leave him alone even in Medīna and invaded the town. They tried to incite the Jews of Medīna against him. Under the circumstances, which I have just briefly described, if war ensues and the victim has a chance for reprisal, an attempt is made to requite oppression with oppression. It is said that all is fair in war. However, our Prophet[sa] established high standards of compassion and mercy even in these situations. It had been a very short time that they had left the relentless persecution of Mecca, the memories of which were still raw; the Holy Prophet[sa] was mindful of the pain of his adherents more than his own pain, yet he did not breach the Islamic rules and regulations. He did not contravene his inherent high morals that constituted his teachings. You may notice the extent to which certain Western countries go to in treating those with whom they are at war these days, and notice this blessed model in contrast. Regarding this, in history, a tradition is related which is as follows:

At the Battle of Badr, the spot where the Muslim troops had encamped was not very suitable. Ḥubāb bin Mundhar inquired from the Holy Prophet[sa] whether the choice of the area for encampment was by Divine revelation or he had chosen it himself from a strategic point of view. The Holy Prophet[sa] replied that he has chosen it due to its elevation thinking it would be a good place strategically. It was submitted to him that it was not such a good area. They should head for the water spring and take control of it, and make a reservoir there. This way they would have access to water and the enemy would not. The Holy Prophet[sa] accepted this counsel and they moved to that spot and encamped there. After a short while a few people of *Quraish* came by to drink water, the Companions[ra] tried to stop them from getting the water. The Holy Prophet[sa] refrained his Companions[ra] to do so, and said, "Let them take water."

(As-Sīratun-Nabawiyyah libne Hashām, Vol. 2, p. 284, Ghazwatu Badril-Kubrā, Mashwaratul Ḥubāb ʻAlar-Rasūl Ṣallallāhu ʻAlaihi wasallam)

Islam did not spread through the force of the sword. Rather, it spread through good moral behaviour, and the Islamic teachings of freedom of conscience and creed

Such was the high standard of the character of the Holy Prophet[sa] even when dealing with the enemy, who had totally blockaded even the food and drink of the Muslim children just a short while ago. Discounting all that, he did not stop the soldiers belonging to the enemy who had come to get water from the spring, which was under his control because this would have been beneath the moral code. The biggest objection raised against Islam is that it was spread 'with the sword'. The people who had come for the water could have been put under duress for accessing the water and forced to accept their conditions. The pagans fought many battles in this manner. However, this is not what the Holy Prophet[sa] did. It could be said here that maybe this step was taken to gain favour to avoid war because the Muslims were in a weak position. However, this was not the case. The bloodthirsty tendencies of the pagans of Mecca towards the Muslims were common knowledge to all Muslims, therefore no one ever entertained this vain imagination in particular, there was no question that the Holy Prophet[sa] would be under such an illusion. He did so because he was the very personification of compassion and kindness who upheld human values; because it was him indeed who was to give the teaching to appreciate these values.

There is an incident of an enemy of Islam who had received the death penalty. Not only was he pardoned by the Holy Prophet[sa], he was also given the freedom to practice his own religion while staying among the Muslims. His story is as follows:

> ‘Ikramah, son of Abū Jahl, fought wars all his life with the Holy Prophet[sa]. At the time of the victory of Mecca, despite the declaration of amnesty, he attacked some troops and caused bloodshed in the Ka‘bah. It was for his war crimes that he had been given the death penalty. Since, at that time, no one could stand up to the Muslims, therefore, after the victory of Mecca, he ran off towards Yemen to save his life. His wife sought forgiveness for him from the Holy Prophet[sa] who most graciously pardoned him. She then followed her husband to fetch him back. ‘Ikramah could not believe that he had been pardoned despite the fact that he had meted out such cruelty, killed so many Muslims and was fighting till the last day, how could he be forgiven? However, she somehow managed to convince him and brought him back. When ‘Ikramah came in the presence of the Holy Prophet[sa] he wanted to have confirmation of his clemency. On his arrival the Holy Prophet[sa] made an amazing gesture of goodwill, and stood up as a mark of respect for him in his capacity as the leader of the enemy. On his asking he told ‘Ikramah that he had indeed pardoned him.
>
> (Mu’aṭṭā’ Imam Mālik, Kitābun-Nikāḥ, Nikāḥul Mushriki Idhā Aslamat zaujatuhū qablahū)

'Ikramah inquired if his pardon was on the grounds that he stayed firm on his own faith? That he had not embraced Islam, and he still maintained his idolatrous stance, was he still forgiven? Confirmation of this by the Prophet[sa] moved 'Ikramah immensely and he cried out, 'O Muḥammad! Certainly, you are extremely forbearing, compassionate and benevolent to your kindred.' Seeing the miracle of the supreme civility and act of kindness of the Holy Prophet[sa] 'Ikramah embraced Islam.

(As-Sīratul-Ḥalbiyyah,Volume 3, p 109, Bābu Dhikri Maghāziyāti Ṣallallāhu 'alaihi wasallam , Fatḥi Makkata Sharrafahallāhu Ta'ālā, Printed in Beirut)

This is the manner in which Islam was spread; with excellent manners and with freedom of conscience and religion. The act of supreme civility and freedom of religion had a person like 'Ikramah smitten in a moment. The Holy Prophet[sa] had even afforded prisoners and slaves the freedom of religion, while maintaining that the propagation of Islam was in accordance with the Divine commandment to spread the teachings of Islam to those who did not know about it. The purpose behind it was to grant nearness of God to others, and it was done out of sympathy for others.

An incident about one of the prisoners is related as follows:

Sa'īd bin Abī Sa'īd narrates that he heard Ḥaḍrat Abū Huraira[ra] say that when the Holy Prophet[sa] sent an expedition to *Najad*, a person from the tribe of *Banū*

Ḥanīfah, named Thumāmah bin Athāl, was brought in as aprisoner. The Companions[ra] tied him to a pillar of the Prophet's[sa] Mosque. The Holy Prophet[sa] came to him and inquired, 'O Thumāmah, what is your excuse or what do you think will be done with you?' He replied, 'I have a positive expectation. If you have me killed, you will be killing a murderer. If you show me goodwill, you will be, favouring a person who values kindness. If you want property you may have as much as you like.' His people could give property for him. The next day, the Holy Prophet[sa] again came by and asked Thumāmah what did he wish? He replied that he had already said the previous day that if a favour was bestowed on him it would be a favour on a person who valued kindness. The Holy Prophet[sa] left him there. On the third day he returned and inquired, 'O Thumāmah, What are your intentions?' He said that he had already said what he had to say. The Holy Prophet[sa] ordered that Thumāmah be freed. Thumāmah went to a nearby date orchard and bathed there, he re-entered the mosque and recited the *Shahādah* and said, 'O Muḥammad[sa] by God I disliked your face the most in the world, but now it is so that your face is the most beloved to me. By God, I disliked your faith the most, but now it is so that my most beloved faith is the one you have brought. By God, I disliked your town the most, but now this is my most beloved town. Your horse-riders held me although I wanted to perform *Umrah*. What do you say about this?' The Holy Prophet[sa] gave him the glad-tiding, congratulated him for accepting Islam and ordered him to perform *Umrah*, saying that Allah would accept it. When he reached Mecca someone asked him if he had become a

Sabian. He replied, 'No, I have believed in Muḥammad[sa], Prophet of God and by God, now not even a grain of wheat shall come your way from Yamāmah.

(Ṣaḥīḥ Bukhārī, Kitābul-Maghāzī, Bābu Wafdi Banī Ḥanīfah wa Ḥadīthu Thumāmah bin Athāl)

Another tradition relates that he was either beaten up or an attempt was made to beat him on which he had said that no grain would come and this would not happen until permission was given by the Holy Prophet[sa]. As a result, he went back to his people, and the grain export was stopped. The situation got quite bad. Eventually Abū Sufyān took a plea to the Holy Prophet[sa] saying that people were starving, and asked for some pity to be shown to his people. The Holy Prophet[sa] did not say you would only get the grain if you accepted Islam. Rather, he promptly sent a message to Thumāmah to stop the embargo as it was cruel. The young, the elderly, the sick needed food and it should be available for them.

(As-Sīratul-Nabawiyyah, Ibni Hashām 'asru Thumāmatabni Athālil Ḥanafiyyi wa Islamuhu - Khurūjuhu Ilā Makkata wa Qiṣṣatuhū Ma'a Quraishin)

We see that it was not said to the prisoner, Thumāmah, that you are in our control, accept Islam. Rather, he was treated well for three days and then the higher standards of treatment were established in that he was released. Thumāmah too had the insight that as soon as he was given the freedom he presented himself for the subjugation of the Holy Prophet[sa] knowing full well that his worldly and spiritual welfare was indeed in this subjugation. Likewise, the Holy Prophet[sa] did not coerce a Jewish slave into doing what he wished just because he was under his authority. The man fell very ill and when the Prophet[sa] saw that his life was in danger he was concerned for his good ending. He was concerned that he should not depart this world without accepting the final *Sharia* of God, so that he may be forgiven by God. He went to visit him on his sick bed and asked him most affectionately to accept Islam.

Ḥaḍrat Anas[ra] narrates that:

> The Holy Prophet[sa] had a Jewish slave who fell ill. The Holy Prophet[sa] went to visit him and asked him to accept Islam. Another tradition relates that he [the Jew] looked at his elders; anyhow, whether on being given the permission or of his own accord, he accepted Islam.
>
> (Ṣaḥīḥ Bukhārī, Kitābul-Janā'iz, Bābu 'Idhā aslamaṣṣabiyyu famāta ... Hadith No. 1356)

This acceptance was certainly borne out of the loving and affectionate treatment given to this young man when he was a slave; he must have realised that certainly Islam was a true religion and that there was salvation in accepting it. He would have never imagined that an embodiment of affection and love such as the Holy Prophet[sa] was, would ever think of anything bad for him. Certainly, he[sa] was on the truth and always called others to what was the best, and always advised about what was the best. Such was the freedom that he had established and there can be no (other such) example of this in the world.

The Holy Prophet[sa] preferred freedom of conscience, freedom of religion, and freedom in life even before his claim to prophethood and he disliked slavery. When after marriage Ḥaḍrat Khadījah[ra] handed over all her property and her slaves to him, he said to her that if she was giving it all to him, it would all be at his disposal to do as he pleased. She said that is why she was giving these to him. He said he would free the slaves. She replied that he could do as he pleased, once she had given it all to him, she had no influence over it and that it was now his property. The Holy Prophet[sa] immediately called all of Ḥaḍrat Khadījah's[ra] slaves and told them that they were free from that day onwards. He also distributed a large portion of the property among the poor and the needy.

Among the slaves he freed, one was called Zaid. It seems that he was brighter than the rest of the slaves and was intelligent. He realised it well that once he was granted freedom, the stigma of slavery had been removed, however his well-being was in permanently remaining in the subjugation of the Holy Prophet[sa].

Therefore, he said:

> Very well, you have freed me, however, I shall not go, I shall stay with you as your slave. He stayed on with the Holy Prophet[sa] and their mutual love and affection continued to grow. Zaid, who was originally from a

well-to-do family, had been kidnapped [as a child] and then sold on by the bandits. He was sold several times over and had eventually reached here. His parents and other relatives were ever looking for him and came to know that their son was in Mecca. They reached Mecca and having found out their son's whereabouts came to the Holy Prophet[sa]. They offered him as much wealth as he wanted for the freedom of their son, saying his mother was desperately aggrieved. The Holy Prophet[sa] told them that he had already freed Zaid so he was free to go, and that he did not want any money. His people asked him to come. However, the son replied, 'I have met with you and this is sufficient, if an opportunity comes by, I shall meet my mother as well, however, I cannot come with you people now. I am now the slave of the Prophet[sa] and there is no question of separation from him. I love the Prophet[sa] more than one could love one's mother and father.' Zaid's father and uncles urged him but he refused to go. Seeing the love of Zaid, the Holy Prophet[sa] said, 'Zaid was already free but from today he is my son.' Zaid's father and uncles left for their homeland while Zaid remained there permanently.

(Abstracted from Dībāchah Tafsīr-ul-Qur'an, Mirzā Bashīr-ud-Dīn Maḥmūd Aḥmad, p. 112)

After prophethood, the Holy Prophet's[sa] values of freedom were further enhanced. Besides his inherent good nature he had the directive of the *Sharia* revealed to him that gave the slaves their rights, and if one could not fulfil them then one had to set them free.

A tradition recounts that once a Companion[ra] was beating up his slave which the Holy Prophet[sa] happened to see. He expressed great anger. On this the Companion[ra] freed his slave. The Holy Prophet[sa] remarked that if he had not freed the slave he would have come under the chastisement of God.

(Ṣaḥīḥ Muslim, Kitābul Īmān, Bābu Ṣuḥbatil mamālīki .... Hadith No. 4308)

So this is what freedom is!

An example of freedom of expression for people of other religions can be found during the times when the Prophet's[sa] government was established in Medīna.

In a tradition, Ḥaḍrat Abū Huraira[ra] narrates that two men were quarrelling. One was a Muslim and the other a Jew. The Muslim said, 'I swear by that Being Who chose Muḥammad[sa] over all the worlds and granted him excellence over others.' The Jew retorted, 'I swear by that Being Who granted excellence to Moses over all the worlds and chose him.'

On this the Muslim slapped the Jew. The Jew took the complaint to the Holy Prophet[sa], who asked the Muslim for the details and then said:

لَا تُخَيِّرُوْنِیْ عَلٰی مُوْسٰی

Do not give me preference over Moses.

(Ṣaḥīḥ Bukhārī, Kitābul-Khuṣūmāti, Bābu mā yudhkaru fil-Ashkhāṣi wal-Khuṣūmati bainal-Muslimi wal-Yahūdī)

Thus was his standard of freedom, religious freedom and freedom of conscience, during his reign. After the migration to Medīna, the Holy Prophet[sa] entered into a pact with the Jews and other tribes to maintain peace. Due to the Muslims being in the majority, either by themselves or by including those who although were not Muslim but had joined them, the government was in the hands of the Holy Prophet[sa]. However, this did not entail that the feelings of others were not looked after. Despite the Qur'ānic testimony that he indeed had excellence over all the other Prophets, he did not tolerate a contest over Prophets that could have polluted the atmosphere. After hearing what the Jew had said, he only reproached the Muslim not to involve Prophets in their quarrels. His stance being that it was well and good that the Muslim considered him most excellent among all Prophets, that God too gave testimony to this. Yet the feelings of a person in their realm could not be hurt because of something that was said about his Prophet. He would not allow this. If one was to hold him in respect one had to hold other Prophets in respect as well. So, these were the standards of justice and freedom of expression of the Prophet[sa], which he had established to look after the feelings of his own as well as the others. At times, preference was given to the sentiments of others.

Practical examples of the conduct of the Holy Prophet[sa] with regard to establishment of human values and religious tolerance

There is another example of his establishment of human values and of fairness.

'Abdur Raḥmān bin abī Laila narrates that Sahl bin Ḥanīf and Qaiṣ bin Sa'd were sitting at a place called *Qādsia* when a funeral procession went by. They both stood up. When they were told that the funeral was that of a non-Muslim, they replied:

> Once a funeral procession went by the Holy Prophet[sa] who stood up as a mark of respect. He was told that it was the funeral of a Jew. To this the Holy Prophet[sa] replied:
>
> اَلَيْسَتْ نَفْسًا
>
> Was he not human?
>
> (Ṣaḥīḥ Bukhārī, Kitābul-Janā'iz, Bābu man qāma lijanāzati yahūdī)

Thus should be the respect for the religion of others as well as for humanity. Such expressions and such models create an atmosphere of religious tolerance. In conveying such feelings, kind sentiments for others are generated and it is these sentiments that create an atmosphere of love and peace. Unlike the actions of the worldly people of today that are nothing beyond creating an atmosphere of hatred.

Another Tradition relates that at the victory of Khaybar some Muslims came upon some copies of the Torah. The Jews went to the Holy Prophet[sa] and requested that their Holy Book be returned to them. The Holy Prophet[sa] directed the Companions[ra] to return the religious books of the Jews to them.

(As-Sīratul-Ḥalabiyyah, Bābu Dhikri Maghāziyyati Ṣallallāhu 'Alaihi Wasallam ... Gazwah Khaibar, Vol. 3, p. 49)

Despite the wrong attitude of the Jews for which they were being punished, the Holy Prophet[sa] did not tolerate to even treat the enemy in a way that would have hurt their religious sentiments.

These are some isolated incidents that I have related. I also mentioned that a pact was made in Medīna, I will now recount the clauses of this pact that have reached us through the Traditions, and expound how the Prophet[sa] made efforts to create an atmosphere of tolerance in that environment, and how he aspired to bring peace in that setting. So that peace was established and dignity of humanity was upheld in the society.

- Some conditions of the pact that he made with the Jews upon reaching Medīna were that Muslims and Jews would live with mutual sympathy and sincerity, and would refrain from oppression against each other. Despite the fact that the Jews continually breached this clause, the Holy Prophet[sa] continued to treat them with kindness, until the time the matter reached to such an extreme that he was forced to take severe actions againstthe Jews.

- The second condition was that each people would have religious freedom. Despite the Muslims being in the majority the others were free to practice their religion.

- The third condition was that the life and property of all inhabitants would be safe and would be respected, unless someone committed a crime or transgression. In this matter too there would be no discrimination, whether the criminal was a Muslim or a non-Muslim, punishment would be given anyhow. Additionally, protection was to be a mutual task. It was to be the government's task.

All sort of disagreements would be brought to the Holy Prophet[sa] for decision and each decision would be made in accordance with the respective people's own religious law. As the Holy Prophet[sa] was the Commander-in-Chief at the time, all cases were to be presented to him anyhow. Objections are now raised by Christians and other opponents that the decisions given for some Jews, which were in accordance with their own *Sharia*, were too harsh. Although they were carried out according to the stipulated conditions.

- Another condition was that no one would go to war without the permission of the Holy Prophet[sa]. It was, therefore, important to abide by this condition while living under the government. The Jihadī organisations of today could take guidance from this clause. Any kind of Jihad is not allowed without the permission of the government of the country except in the situation that one joins the armed forces of the government and in the event the country goes to war, they also get to participate.

- Another condition was that if any nation fought against the Jews or the Muslims, they would help each other, and in the case of a truce with the enemy if the Muslims or the non-Muslims attained any war booty or any other benefit from the truce then this would be proportionally shared by all. Similarly, if Medīna was attacked all will join forces to contend with it.

- Another condition was that the Jews would not give the Quraish of Mecca or their associates any kind of help or refuge as it was the Meccans who had forced the Muslims out of there. The Muslims had found refuge here [in Medīna], therefore, those who lived under this government could not enter into any pact with the enemy nation or take any help from them. It was stated that each nation would meet its own expenses. In accordance with this pact no oppressor or offender or insurgent would be safe from punishment or retribution. As mentioned before, whoever committed an act of oppression, iniquity, or wrongdoing, would be seized and punished without any discrimination of being a Muslim or a Jew or another.

(Abstracted from Sīrat Khātamun-Nabiyyīn[sa], Mirzā Bashīr Aḥmad, p. 279)

It was to promote this very religious freedom and tolerance that the Holy Prophet[sa] permitted the visiting Christians from *Najrān* to worship inside the Prophet's[sa] Mosque. They worshipped while they were facing eastward. The Companions[ra] were of the opinion that this should not have been allowed, but the Holy Prophet[sa] said:

It does not matter.

The Letter of Immunity that the Holy Prophet[sa] gave to the people of *Najrān* is also reported, in which it is mentioned that he[sa] had undertaken the responsibility of protection of the boundaries of the Christians (who had come from *Najrān*) by the Muslim Army. Furthermore, it was also the obligation of the Muslims to protect their Churches, places of worship and inns, no matter how far off they were located, and whether they were in cities, mountains or woods. They were free to worship in accordance with their religion, and to safeguard their freedom of worship was also the responsibility of the Muslims.

The Holy Prophet[sa] said:

Since they are now the subjects of a Muslim government and so are my subjects, therefore, their protection is obligatory upon me. The pact goes on to state that the Muslims would not include them (the Christians) in their battle expeditions without their willingness. Their priests and religious leaders would not be removed from their positions and would continue their tasks. There would be no interference in their places of worship. These would not be brought to any use under any circumstances, and would not be converted into inns. These would not be used as accommodation for anyone and would not be used for any other purpose without permission. *Jizyah* would not be collected from religious scholars and priests no matter where they were. If a Muslim had a Christian wife, she would have total freedom of worship in her own way. If anyone wished to go to their own religious scholars for advice, they could do so. With regard to repairs of Churches, etc., the pact maintained that if they sought financial help and moral support from the Muslims, they should help them as it was a preferred option. It would neither be deemed a loan nor a favour but would be a means to enhance the pact in that it would improve social connections, and spirit of mutual help.

(Abstracted from Zādul Ma'ādi Fī Khairil 'Ibādī, Faṣlu Fī Qudūmi Wafdi Najrāna ...)

With standards of religious freedom and tolerance of the Holy Prophet[sa] as these, it is extremely cruel to allege that Islam was spread through force and oppression.

The Promised Messiah[as] states:

At a time when the People of the Book and the idolaters of Mecca were extremely depraved and having committed a wicked act considered they had done a meritorious act. They did not desist from crime, and interfered with public order. Allah the Exalted willed to save the helpless from their clutches by giving the reins of government into the hands of the Holy Prophet[sa]. Since the land of Arabia was unbridled and the people were not under the rule of any King, consequently each faction lived its life most freely and daringly. The people exceeded in crime day by day as no law of punishment existed for them. So, God had mercy on this land ... and sent the Holy Prophet[sa] not only as a Prophet for this land but also made him the King of the land, and completed the Holy Qur'an as such a law that contained all directives pertaining to judicial, criminal and financial matters. Therefore, the Holy Prophet[sa] was the ruler of all factions in his capacity as the King and people of all religions brought their matters to him for judgment.

It is proven from the Holy Qur'an that once a matter between a Muslim and a Jew was brought to the court of the Prophet[sa] for judgment. After investigations the Holy Prophet[sa] deemed the Jew rightful and decreed against the claim the Muslim had made.

Thus, some unwise opponents who do not read the Holy Qur'an attentively, consider every aspect under the sphere of prophethood of the Holy Prophet[sa], while punishments such as these were given under the auspices of Khilāfat. That is, it is an obligation of a government.

He[as] goes on to state:

> After Ḥaḍrat Mūsā[as], the Israelites had separate Prophets and Kings. The Kings kept peace and order through the political process. However, at the time of the Holy Prophet[sa], both these offices were granted by God to the Prophet[sa]. Excluding the criminals, how the rest were treated is quite clear from the following verse:
>
> وَقُلْ لِّلَّذِيْنَ اُوْتُوا الْكِتٰبَ وَالْاُمِّيّٖنَ ءَاَسْلَمْتُمْ ط فَاِنْ اَسْلَمُوْا
> فَقَدِ اهْتَدَوْا ج وَاِنْ تَوَلَّوْا فَاِنَّمَا عَلَيْكَ الْبَلٰغُ ط [15]
>
> (Al-Juzw No. 3, Sūrah Āl-e-'Imrān)
>
> This verse does not declare that it is also your task to battle with them. It is evident from this that war was only meant for the criminal minded people who killed the Muslims, created disorder in the public, and were engaged in theft and robbery. These wars were fought in the capacity of a King and not in the capacity of prophethood. As Allah the Exalted declares:
>
> وَقَاتِلُوْا فِيْ سَبِيْلِ اللّٰهِ الَّذِيْنَ يُقَاتِلُوْنَكُمْ وَلَا تَعْتَدُوْا ط

---

15. And say to those who have been given the Book and to the unlearned, 'Have you submitted?' If they submit, then they will surely be guided; but if they turn back, then thy duty is only to convey the message. (Sūrah Āl-e-'Imrān, 3:21)

إِنَّ اللّٰهَ لَا يُحِبُّ الْمُعْتَدِيْنَ ○ [16]

(Al-Juzw No. 2, Sūrah Al-Baqarah)

(Chashma-e-Ma'rifat, Rūḥānī Khazā'in, vol. 23, pp. 242-243)

How could it be that a Prophet as holy as him[sa], to whom this *Sharia* was revealed, would contravene the directives that were Divinely revealed to him? Indeed, he had declared general amnesty at the victory of Mecca without the clause that protection was conditional on accepting Islam. We have heard of one example of this. This amnesty had different clause that protection was conditional on accepting Islam. We have heard of one example of this. This amnesty had different facets but did not include the acceptance of Islam as a prerequisite for pardon. Amnesty was declared for going to and entering different places, for coming under certain banners, by entering the Ka'bah and by going to certain houses. This was, such a great example, the like of which cannot be seen anywhere else. An unqualified announcement was made that:

لَا تَثْرِيْبَ عَلَيْكُمُ الْيَوْمَ ط

No blame *shall lie* on you this day. (Sūrah Yūsuf, 12:93)

---

16. And fight in the cause of Allah against those who fight against you, but do not transgress. Surely, Allah loves not the transgressors. (Sūrah Al-Baqarah, 2:191).

A thousand salutations and blessings on him[sa] who set these excellent examples and granted us such a teaching. May we also be enabled by Allah the Exalted to act upon it.